AF488428

Additional Praise for *Dear 1L*

"*Dear 1L* is the mentor every student deserves as they take on 1L year. Amanda divulges all the tricks to help you avoid mistakes on the things lawyers know but never explain until you have already gotten them wrong. Every law student needs *Dear 1L* in their corner rooting for them. It's an absolute must-read." —**Jordana Confino, Positive Lawyer, Former Law School Assistant Dean of Professionalism, Founder of JC Coaching & Consulting**

"Each time I read *Dear 1L*, I discover something new that I might not have picked up the last time. This book goes beyond pre-law, law school, and legal practice, because it offers valuable advice for navigating challenges at any stage in life. I feel completely prepared to apply to law school and know what to expect there having read this!" —**Diliana Gresbrink, Boston University (BA 2025)**

"*Dear 1L* is a daily pep talk from a trusted mentor, coach, cheerleader, and friend. Every first-year law student needs that. Amanda Haverstick artfully untangles fears, worries, stressors, and anxieties that inevitably infiltrate the law school experience, while offering practical advice on how to step into the legal writing arena with fortitude. This book will change 1L lives for the better." —**Heidi K. Brown, Author of *The Introverted Lawyer*, *Untangling Fear in Lawyering*, and *The Flourishing Lawyer***

Dear 1L

Notes to Nurture a New Legal Writer

Amanda Dealy Haverstick

For Dad

Dear Reader,

Thank you for picking up my book! Collected inside are the letters, checklists, and other tips I've posted on LinkedIn for law students and legal writers since 2021. I have edited much of the original content, and you'll also find new material throughout.

The book is arranged chronologically and by topic for you:

- Part I contains material for before law school;
- Parts II and III cover 1L fall and spring terms; and
- Part IV will help with your job applications.

You will find the book particularly helpful for 1L legal writing. You'll need to complete several assignments for that writing course, including an objective "office memo" in the fall, and an advocacy brief in the spring. These will count for almost all of your final grade.

In your 1L "doctrinal" classes, moreover, you'll have final exams that require you to write several "IRAC essays." You'll also need a professional job-application packet to secure a summer internship and a full-time role after law school. The material in this book is designed to prepare you for and help you perform all of these written tasks well.

When all is said and done, writing will be the common thread that runs through every aspect of how you perform in the first year of law school. You'll also use your writing skills no matter what you do with your degree. Too many students don't learn the right way to write about the law the first time around. This book is my effort to help change that.

I also aim to welcome you into the world of legal writing in a warm environment where you feel like you're learning tips from a friend, not being lectured by a law-school professor or the author of a serious book about grammar and legal doctrine. Legal writing is hard. Learning about it shouldn't be.

Finally, you may wonder what makes me a reliable source of information on these topics. You'll find a bit about me next, and then we'll dive right into Chapter 1.

See you inside.

Amanda
March 2024

A Bit About Me

Since we're going to be spending some time together in the up-coming pages, I thought you might want to know who is writing to you. So here goes.

I'm fifty-four, female, and married to Matt for twenty-five years (he's a lawyer, too). We live in a suburb of Philadelphia and have three daughters, including one who started law school during the years I wrote this book.

I grew up in a suburb of NYC. My father was a lawyer and my mother, an English teacher. (Yes, I know; go figure.) The rest is pretty much resume stuff:

- I was a paralegal at a big firm in Boston for two years be-tween college and law school (Harvard, BA 1991; Boston College, JD 1996).
- After law school, I worked as a labor and employment law attorney for twenty years, primarily at two big firms in NYC and Philadelphia (Proskauer & Morgan Lewis) and as in-house counsel at The Hershey Company.
- In 2016, I retired from active practice and took several years to be at home with my family before I started a busi-ness coaching legal writing in 2021.

Also in 2021, I started mentoring law students and writing letters to them on LinkedIn. This book is the product of those writings. All of it has brought me more fulfillment than I ever could have imagined.

In my free time, I like to play board and card games, dance to fun music, and travel with my family. I also love meeting and talking to new students, so if you'd like to learn more about my community, please reach out!

Here's where you can find me:

- through my website, Dear1L.com
- on LinkedIn at https://www.linkedin.com/in/amandahaverstick/
- by email, Amanda@Dear1L.com

~Amanda
March 2024

Contents

Expanded Contents

PART III: 1L SPRING

Ch 8   **January Jump-Start**

DEAR 1L

PART I: PRE-LAW SUMMER

1.1 Pre-law prep

When I started tutoring law students in 2021, I began searching for resources to help me get better at helping them. When my daughter then decided to apply to law school, I doubled down on my research. I also asked for advice from law students and lawyers on LinkedIn:

- What recommendations did folks have?
- What should she do in the summer to prepare for law school?

What follows are eight tips distilled from my research and the responses I received. I hope you'll find them helpful.

TIP 1: Enjoy it!

"Relax and have fun" dominates the discussion on pre-law prep, and rightly so. You're going to be working hard in the fall, and your schedule will feel more programmed and regimented than you're used to. Fill up your pre-law fuel tank with memories from carefree, lazy days surrounded by family and friends.

TIP 2: Train for what's ahead.

Getting in shape is another widely touted suggestion. You're about to enter a nine-month trial. It will be physical, mental, emotional, and psychological. It may also be the most intense competition you've experienced thus far.

If you were an athlete or musician, would you show up to your most important performance without advance training? Of course not. So don't show up for law school that way. You want to be at your strongest coming into the fall.

This is my #1 tip that can make a difference in your academic success. I am convinced that my own pre-law regimen was the key to mine. (See additional discussion in chapter 1.2.)

TIP 3: Get your affairs in order.

Take care of:

- doctor's appointments,

- medication refills,
- contact lenses,
- housing arrangements,
- school supplies, etc.

You will have much less time for these types of things once law school starts.

Insider Recommendation: Get your textbooks as soon as you can once you know your professors. Watch for important email announcements from your school.

There are also some great Facebook groups where 2Ls and 3Ls post used books for sale, and most law schools have book exchanges, as well, so look around to get the best prices. That said, past students have also counseled against spending tons of time searching for bargain used books, because reading may be due for 1L on Day 1.

TIP 4: Read.

Reading is a fabulous thing to do to get your brain in tune for the reading during 1L. On the other hand, one might argue that you should rest your brain.

If you enjoy reading (unlike me), try to read well-written prose. That you read matters more than what you read. The key is to hone your concentration skills, even if you're reading "junk."

While you're at it though, you might as well read something that will help you in law school.

You've taken a key first step in reading this book, and I've listed some additional titles for you in Appendix A.

Corollaries to Tip 4:

a. Learn and practice speed-reading/skimming skills.

b. Invest in a good reading light. (I ruined my eyes in law school. So, so stupid in retrospect.)

c. Read what your professors have written—books, briefs, articles, anything. Then, when you are writing your brief or taking an exam for that professor, use their words, parrot their phrasing, and mimic their style. If you write in your reader's language, they're more likely to like what they read. This approach is time consuming, but if you really want to get ahead before law school starts, give it a try as soon as you know your professors. You'll certainly have more time for additional reading now than you will once classes start.

TIP 5: Line up some go-to podcasts.

When you get tired from reading—and you will in the year ahead—you'll want to have some ready podcasts to turn to. That way, you can keep learning even when your eyes simply cannot look at another word. And if you commute to and from law school, podcast-listening may be your game changer.

Former law students give these three their highest marks.

1. *The Law School Toolbox* podcast is well-rounded, talking about everything from law-school exams to what you should wear on your first day of school. I'd start here, as you'll find material relevant to the summer before law school.

2. *How I Lawyer.* Check out episodes 29 and 31 to start, as they cover content specifically meant for 1Ls.

3. *Law to Fact.* I haven't listened to this one personally, but students laud it profusely for learning legal theory. You might save this one for when law school starts.

There are infinite others, so please do your own research for pods that suit your style, but I hope these three can get you started.

TIP 6: Prepare your friends and family.

One thing to expect is that you'll be a bit off the grid this upcoming year, especially at the beginning.

It's important to ensure that your family and friends "get" this reality early, because you'll need their unconditional support throughout. I doubt any lawyer, 2L, or 3L would deny feeling some degree of overwhelm during the first semester of law school. Most 1Ls find themselves:

- less available to chat by phone or text (or whatever app) than before, and less available than what your family and friends may expect; and

- less able to attend so many social events with non-law school friends. (You'll make many new friends, though, and some will become lifelong besties.)

Unless your current friends and family members have been through 1L before, they may not understand. Many non-law people think of the first year of law school as "just another year in college." It is not.

Unlike college, 1L can feel more like studying abroad or doing some sort of intense boot camp. Don't be scared by that: It's going to be wonderful. You'll remember the start of 1L forever. But you will make the transition much more smoothly if you've got your greatest supporters ready and willing to support you, even when you have less availability to give back.

All that said, I've found it's the students with children and families of their own who often manage better. Yes, it's an insane juggling act (I remember from many years in BigLaw with three little ones), but somehow having more things that have to get done can make you more efficient than having less to do. Remember, work expands to fill the time allotted for its completion.

But whatever your particular family situation, knowing that it's going to be different and planning ahead, and getting everyone on the same page about expectations can really make things run more smoothly once school starts.

TIP 7: Get on LinkedIn, start networking, and prepare for your job search.

No, it is not too early. A prime reason you're going to law school is to get a good job afterwards.

- Prepare a solid LinkedIn profile and start talking to lawyers.
- Reach out and learn from 2Ls, 3Ls, and alumni from your school.
- Prepare an updated resume in the proper format, and gather references you can list.

Avoid last-minute scrambling this fall and winter, when applications for 1L summer jobs start. You have FAR more free time now than you will then!

TIP 8: Hone your writing skills.

When you write about abstract legal doctrine—the way you will be doing in law school—your sentences will be unintelligible if not written correctly. The littlest comma can make all the difference in the world when it comes to a court's interpretation of text. I cannot impress upon you enough how critical it is for you to have the basics down cold.

Refresh and hone your skills this summer. The investment will pay off in spades—in 1L and beyond.

1.2 Try my three-point, high-energy plan

For reasons I'll share with you at some point, I stumbled into a really good regimen for 1L that I began the summer before. If I could write a prescription for what I did, it would say this:

1. Start and keep a full-night-of-sleep policy.

Please don't be one of those 1Ls who "plays things by ear" when it comes to getting enough sleep each night. You can't afford to be less than your very, very best.

To maximize your chance of success, start a non-negotiable, full-night-of-sleep schedule, and start it now. (You'll likely need to practice and get acclimated so you can hit the ground running on 1L Day 1.)

For me, the ideal was 8 or 9 PM to 5 AM. That way, I got eight to nine full hours with several hours free in the early morning to exercise and study before my 10 AM class. I also found the early morning to be the very best time to do my reading.

- There are fewer distractions.
- Your eyes and brain are well rested.
- You'll read faster and retain material better than the night before.

This was a typical Mon–Tues schedule for me:

Mon

5 AM	Wake, coffee
6:00	Gym cardio, shower
7:30	Breakfast at school
8–10	Library (two hours reading)
10–11:15	Contracts
11:30–12:45	Torts
12:45	Lunch
1–3	Library (two hours reading)
3–4:15	Legal Research and Writing
5:00	Dinner
6–8	TV/relax/any extra reading
9 PM	Lights out

Tues

5 AM	Wake, coffee
6:00	Gym cardio, shower
7:30	Breakfast at school
8–10	Library (two hours reading)
10–11:45	Civil Procedure
12:00	Lunch
12:30–2:30	Library (two hours reading)
2:30–4	Meetings/Office Hours
5:00	Dinner
6–8	TV/relax/any extra reading
9 PM	Lights out

Obviously, adjust for your own schedule. If you are a part-time, online, or night student, the hours I kept in law school will not be anything like yours. Some of you will have family constraints or other circumstances that dictate which hours you do what.

But whatever schedule you choose, try to have a solid chunk of time as near as possible to your first class of the day, and get some work done early.

The science on this is beyond debate: Sleep is a superpower. Why would anyone try to do law school without it?

2. Get on a meal plan.

This may sound silly, but one thing I did during 1L weekdays that really helped me was to eat the same thing for breakfast and lunch each day, at roughly the same time each day.

During those time blocks, I sat alone and did my reading for the classes coming up later that same day. A humdrum culinary and antisocial existence? Perhaps. But a small, short-term sacrifice. (And I more than made up for it on weekends.)

By making this sacrifice, moreover, I accomplished two key things.

First, I eliminated two daily decisions. Over the course of the academic year, that was ten decisions per week and more than 100 decisions per semester.

Decision fatigue is real. The fewer decisions you have to make—even about small things—the better you'll conserve precious energy for focus. And when you're a 1L, every energy source counts.

Why include more than 100 daily decisions to make?

Second, my prearranged meal plan meant I got my readings done early in the day. Because I, like most, tend to focus better earlier in the day, and because fewer distractions interfere then (especially at breakfast time), I had a greater ability to extract the important points from the reading quickly. I avoided getting bogged down in the slow, word-for-word reading I typically resorted to at night.

I thus read much faster when I did it early in the day.

So consider streamlining your daily meal time. Even if you're not someone who succumbs to internal morality debates about what you "should" eat at any given meal, you can see benefits from removing what-to-eat decisions and using that time productively.

The above takes discipline, but you just have to make it weekdays. Might it be worth the investment?

3. Map your days.

There are many ways to win at 1L. You need a plan that works for you, or you won't stick to it. But all seem to agree that breaking each day into time blocks helps maximize efficiency.

The How-To: You designate specific time ranges on your daily calendar for preparing for and studying after each course. After that, you only worry about the task assigned to the time block you're in. During that block, think of nothing else.

The Benefits: Scheduling time blocks in advance has many benefits. One is that it removes counterproductive transitions after one task is complete.

For example, let's say it's 7:20 PM, and you've just finished your Torts reading. What will you do next? What *should* you do next?

Those are debilitating questions that sap energy. Have all those questions answered in advance. Then, don't think; just do.

For similar reasons, many students cook meals for the week on weekends and do things like lay out their clothing for the next day on weeknights. You'll want to set up all your systems for these types of things before law school starts.

Fewer decisions = more mental energy saved
More energy saved = less fatigue
Less fatigue = better productivity

Won't you give time blocking a try?

1.3 Ten ways to become a better legal writer

A recent remark by a BigLaw partner stopped me dead in my tracks. On a LinkedIn post about legal writing (not mine), he commented:

> "This is what I tell my firm's associates: I don't have the time to teach you how to write by going over your draft with you and explaining why certain parts are good or bad, and why I revised or rewrote certain sections.
>
> Rather, if your product was a pretty good starting point, I revised it to make it better, silently decided whether to send you future work, and then kept moving forward— all without having a teachable moment with you."

Yikes! Is this really what it's come to?

I have a whole lot to say, but my chief takeaway for you is this:

1. In 2024 and beyond, if you want to become a better legal writer, YOU need to take the lead.

That's Step 1, and it's non-negotiable. Here are nine more steps you can pick and choose from to help jumpstart your learning journey:

2. Grow a thick skin.

The earlier you start taking all feedback as a gift, the faster you'll improve. Resist the tendency to take negative critique personally (even when it's delivered insensitively).

You must remember that for as many years as you've been writing in school, you'll be in kindergarten when it comes to legal writing. Accept that in advance, before law school starts, and start your 1L legal writing course with no preconceived notions about how good a writer you are. You will need to be an eager sponge if you want to get better quickly.

3. Build a reference library.

Start a shelf of go-to resources. I grew up on Bryan Garner, so perhaps I'm biased, but I see his works as the most logical place to start. *Legal Writing in Plain English*, *The Winning Brief*, and *Garner's Modern Legal Usage* should all be on your shelves, and you'll find additional recommendations in Appendix A.

4. Find top writers to emulate.

The best way to learn how to write about the law is to read well-written prose that's been written about the law.

I'd start with the name of one appellate litigator—someone whose writing is highly regarded—and start to read what they've written. (For a list of some of our country's best appellate writers, check out *Point Made* by Ross Guberman (listed in Appendix A).)

5. Become an active reader.

When you read top writers, don't be passive. Notice and learn new ways to combine words, new ways to structure sentences, and other features you see and like.

Then you'll want to start incorporating those new words and writing techniques into your own writing and practice using them.

6. Become an active writer.

Learn as you write, too. Instead of reworking a sentence to avoid words or phrases you're not sure how to use, spell, or punctuate, start looking up how and implement.

Eventually, you'll start using new techniques naturally, without even thinking about them.

7. Write about what you learn.

Keep track of the feedback you receive and the new techniques you find by memorializing them in writing. That will reinforce your learning and also generate a future reference file.

I used to keep a "learning file," where I collected articles and notes to refer back to later.

8. Teach what you learn.

Reinforce what you learn by explaining it to someone else. You never really understand something fully until you try to explain it to someone else. They will ask questions, expose gaps in your thinking, and help you hone what you think you know.

9. Get comfortable with tech.

In this day and age, you simply have no choice but to stay on the cutting edge of new tech tools. Indeed, during the months I was preparing this book, ChatGPT and associated apps started taking the legal-writing world by storm, and for the first fall after this book's preparation, products like Lexis AI+ will be fully integrated into the 1L curriculum.

While further discussion of tech tools is beyond the scope of this book, I encourage you to lean in and start practicing as early and often as possible.

That said, don't spend so much time chasing down new tools that you forget some old standbys. I'll mention just two to start.

First up is Microsoft Word. You'll have to use it for all your legal-writing assignments, both during law school and in your job afterward. How your assignments look will be evaluated along with how they sound. Every year students lose stupid points because they don't know how to adjust their tabs or paragraph spacing. Practice before law school starts. I recommend starting with the tools described in Chapter 11 of Ryan McCarl's 2024 book, *Elegant Legal Writing* (see Appendix A).

Second, start using a thesaurus. My current go-to is OneLook online, but you'll find many from which to choose. In legal writing, getting your words just right will be critical.

10. Work with a coach.

OK, this one's admittedly self-serving, but it can be key—especially to get you started in a personalized, fun, and judgment-free way. Let a coach target the areas where you need work in advance, so you aren't trying to bone up on things like comma placement and pronoun agreement while simultaneously trying to learn complex legal doctrine.

Let's make this the year YOU become a better writer!

CHAPTER 2

Legal Writing 101

2.1 Get ready for a big change

If you want to succeed in 1L legal writing, you'll need to shift your mindset and forget what you did in college. Here are the four big differences to look out for.

1. Length

In college, your papers had to be LONG enough to meet a minimum page or word length (e.g., "must be at least twenty-five pages"). Essentially, you had to keep writing more words to complete the task, and for that, you were rewarded.

But in law school, your memos and briefs must be SHORT enough to fit a page or word maximum (e.g., "must be no more than twelve pages"). If yours goes long, you'll be penalized.

Note that when you're a lawyer, if you file a brief that surpasses the page/word limit, the court may refuse to accept it when you go to file.

I emphasize: At first, you might think writing twelve pages in law school will be faster and easier than writing twenty-five pages in college. It won't be. Learning to say the same thing in fewer words is a skill you'll have to acquire. And it's time consuming.

2. Word and Sentence Style

In college, your professors used big, pedagogical words and abstract phraseology to teach you. The scholars who authored your textbooks did, too.

As a college student, you likely picked up on the trend and started using such language and phrases in your own papers. For that, you were also rewarded.

But in law school, you'll need to cut out all lofty language and phrasing.

Law school rewards basic language:
- little words
- uncomplicated phrasing
- simple sentence structures

Think ninth grade.

3. Complexity

A wise mentor once explained the difference between a college thesis and a legal brief like this to me:

> [W]ith a thesis, you are trying to show that you figured out something really hard. So you effectively say to the reader: there's this really difficult problem, and if you stick with me and follow my reasoning really closely, you'll see how I solved it.
>
> A legal brief is just the opposite. You want to portray the problem as the easiest thing in the world. The right answer is obvious and inevitable: just A, B, C, and then your conclusion is automatic.

Take note of that wholesale shift in approach, and we'll talk more about it inside.

4. Organization of Body Paragraphs

You will also need to forget what you've learned about how to organize a body paragraph.

For high-school and college writing, you likely did something like:

- Topic Sentence
- Explanation
- First Example/Quote
- Second Example/Quote
- Third Example/Quote
- Conclusion

But in legal writing, you must do:

- Conclusion
- Rule
- Explanation
- Analysis
- Conclusion

Legal writing even gives you an acronym for this standard order: CREAC.*

Many law students, myself included, try to fight the system. Please don't do that. You will fail, just like I (almost) did. Lawyers need their paragraphs done in a particular order. The earlier you accept that, the better you'll fare.

(*Note that some legal-writing professors will use different acronyms, such as: (a) the traditional IRAC framework (Issue–Rule–Application/Analysis–Conclusion); (b) TRAC (Thesis–Rule–Analysis–Conclusion); or (c) another variation of CREAC. Try not to get caught up in the differences between acronyms. In the end, they all get you to the same place.)

***

Throughout the course of this book, I will try to help you shift your mindset to legal writing. I'll be popping in at various points in the year to teach you some writing tips that will save you time and help you write better in law school and beyond.

The earlier you start on your journey to improve your writing, the sooner you'll become a better legal writer.

We can aim to make this fun, too!

2.2 Think about your reader

To be a good legal writer, you need to start writing for your reader.

The "law" is complex, abstract, and confusing. For as difficult as it will be for you to construct prose about it, it will be that much more difficult for your reader to understand what you've written. In the end, you will need to do such a good job explaining things that your reader will not only understand what you write, but also agree with it. This reality will inform much of what you need to strive for in your legal writing.

As for who your reader is, it's your professor in the short term, but you should not limit your thinking to your professor. That's partly because your professor is reading with a view to what your future readers will expect from you. And so, yes, follow your professor's rules and writing-style preferences, but beyond that, you should be writing for your future readers.

If you use your 1L projects as writing samples for job applications—as virtually all students do—your readers will be HR coordinators and lawyers at the firms where you apply.

Ultimately, the readers of your legal briefs will include clients, law-firm partners, opposing counsel, law clerks, and judges.

Now, you may think that's a lot of individuals to try to please. But at the end of the day, I don't care who your particular reader is. That's because every single legal reader shares several of the same traits:

- they have something else they could be doing instead of reading what you wrote (so you need to get to the point);
- they are not reading for pleasure, but to extract information (so you need to be clear);
- with the exception of your professor, they will have no clue about your case (so you need to keep your writing simple and designed for education); and
- they are human, so they're inherently prone to boredom and distraction (so you need to be brief).

We'll talk about the three goals you should strive for to make all your readers happy in the next subchapter.

2.3 Aim for three goals

You'll have tons to think about and keep track of when writing this year. Above all else, try to strive for clarity, simplicity, and brevity.

1. Clarity

Clarity is the single most important quality of strong legal writing. Strive for clarity above all else.

If your writing style is confusing, it won't persuade your reader that you know what you're talking about.

More likely, your reader will think that YOU are confused about it.

Here's one way to foster clarity: Don't leave the reader guessing about the identity of your verb subjects.

Do write primarily in the active voice.

2. Simplicity

The law is complex enough as it is. Don't make it more so when you write about it.

Avoid using difficult words with which your reader may be unfamiliar or words with multiple meanings and connotations that could confuse your reader even more.

The same is true for your syntax. Avoid long, intricate sentence structures that require unnecessary concentration to follow.

The more simply you write about something as abstract as the law, the more persuasive you can make your analysis of it.

"Simple" does not mean "simplistic," however. The point isn't to "dumb it down" for the reader, but merely to make your words and sentences facilitate, rather than frustrate, the reader's experience with dense subject matter.

3. Brevity

I doubt any reader has ever finished reading any piece of legal writing and thought, "I am disappointed. I wish it had stretched on for a few more pages."

Consider the late Justice Scalia's remarks during an interview he gave with Bryan Garner:

> Q: "What are the main shortcomings of the briefs that you typically see?"
>
> A: "Prolixity, probably."
>
> —Justice Antonin Scalia, as quoted in Bryan A. Garner, *13 The Scribes Journal of Legal Writing* 53 (2010).

And so...

Do learn the word "prolixity." It's fun to say.

But don't use "prolixity" in legal writing. Stick with simple words.

And don't let "prolixity" be a word that applies to your legal writing. Keep it concise.

2.4 Budget time for the fall memo now

Fall semester would actually be quite manageable if it weren't for the memo you have to write. The memo is NOT something you can pull off in an all-nighter. The sooner you factor in how much of a time suck the memo will be, the better you will do—not only on the memo, but in all your doctrinal exams.

Every year, students procrastinate. They think the memo is just another research paper like they've eked out in the overnight hours immediately before the deadline. THAT WILL NOT WORK OUT WELL. When you get your schedule, you will see the weeks where the memo can consume you. Make a plan now for how you will continue to keep up with your reading and outlining during these weeks.

Otherwise, this time will be lost and never recaptured before exams.

2.5 Lawyers have some wacky ways of writing things

I bet you never thought law school would mean new worries over how to spell basic words and where to put your commas. But it does. And I'm not just talking about Bluebook citations. I'm talking about your prose.

Learn these technical differences early so you don't lose points when it counts.

1. In the legal world, we spell the word "judgment" without an "e."

- Change your Word settings so they autocorrect "judge-ment" to "judgment" when you type.

Although both spellings work in the non-legal context, now that you're joining the legal world, you should probably just start using the "judgment" spelling in everything you write.

2. When typing a court name, we do NOT use superscript.

- Change your settings so the system doesn't superscript the "st," "nd," "rd," or "th" in 1st, 2nd, 3rd, 4th, etc.

3. The word "at" in legal citations is never capitalized.

- Change your settings to stop auto-capitalizing the first letter after you type a period + space.

4. The adjective form of "tort" is "tortious," not "tortuous."

- Change your settings to accept the "tortious" spelling.

There are other words, symbols, and terms that the default Word settings get wrong for legal-writing purposes, but the four above are the ones that come up the most.

***

PS—I have collected these and all my other writing tips in a Global Cheat Sheet for you. See Appendix D.

Grammar tune-up

If someone made a rule that limited what I could teach you about grammar and style in legal writing, and if I were only allowed to share one of my LinkedIn posts with you on the topics, it would probably be this one.

It's a little technical, but it's really that important. Please make sure you "get" it before moving on.

***

You will do much better in legal writing this year if you commit to writing about ACTORS acting, instead of about acts being done.

Before you write your next sentence, think about who is doing what, and start your sentence with the "who" coming first.

Readers associate better with actors than they do with objects or events. By putting the actors first and making them the focus, you'll also avoid the passive voice, its extra words, and its lackluster effect on the reader.

Here's a primer to remind you of some middle school lessons that you likely haven't thought about in a while.

A. How to write in active voice

Identify Subject, Verb, and Object.

- The Subject is the person or entity that carries out the Verb.
- The Object receives the action of the Verb.

To write in active voice, write your sentences with SUBJECT first—then VERB—then OBJECT (if any).

✔ "Plaintiff filed the complaint." (Active)

✘ "The complaint was filed by Plaintiff." (Passive)

If there is no Subject, add it, if you know.

✔ To state a claim, the plaintiff must show a, b, and c. (Active)

✘ These elements must be shown to state a claim: a; b; and c. (Passive)

Don't confuse "passive voice" with "past tense."

Glasses are worn by the woman = passive voice; present tense

Glasses were worn by the woman = passive voice; past tense

B. Benefits of active voice

1. Psycholinguistic studies of brain processes show that a reader's instincts are to expect to see the subject and verb together.

2. Passive voice often sounds weaker. Which would you rather hear?

> "I love you." (Active)
>
> -or-
>
> "You are loved by me." (Passive)

3. Active voice uses fewer words.

- That leads to more concise writing.

4. Active voice uses more precise words.

- That leads to clearer writing.

5. Active voice removes ambiguities.

- That leads to clearer writing.

6. Active voice sounds more confident and direct.

- That leads to more persuasive writing.

C. Using passive voice on purpose

There are any number of reasons to prefer passive voice in a particular sentence. Here are the big two:

1. If you don't know the subject, or the subject is irrelevant, use passive. For example:

> My purse was stolen.
>
> His shoes were made in Italy.
>
> Some of the body's heat is lost through the head.

2. Use passive on purpose when you want to:

> A. emphasize the object or the action;
>
> B. make the sentence flow with those surrounding it; or
>
> C. achieve nuance or effect.

I know that you may feel hesitant when writing about the law. Don't reveal your hesitation by writing passively. You've got people to persuade!

***

PS—OK, enough grammar for a while. We'll pick it up again after law school starts and you're writing your fall memo. :)

PART II: 1L FALL

CHAPTER 3

Getting Your Bearings

3.1 Avoid a "disorientation" week

I wrote the below letter in response to messages from a few students who were contemplating dropping out their first week. Please know that is highly unusual, but it does happen to a few every year.

Although I very much hope you won't need to hear my words on the topic, I include this letter to help you avoid becoming disoriented during the beginning.

***

Dear 1L,

If you're "beyond confused,"

If you think you're "the only one" experiencing self-doubt, or

If you worry everyone else "gets" it when you don't:

FIRST, I am sorry you're experiencing these feelings. The court cases at the beginning of law school can be bewildering.

Please don't let any of the early reading derail your confidence. The court cases from the 1700s are meant for background and historical context.

- They come with arcane terminology and syntax,
- they're inconsistent with one another, and
- you will NOT need to know their details for exams.

Just try to keep up with the reading and follow along in class. No one expects you to be good at this stuff yet.

SECOND, please know that you're not alone. Take a short stroll down the Law School subreddit, and you'll see. Everyone else is baffled, too.

In fact, serious self-doubt—even full-blown imposter syndrome—is experienced by most 1Ls at some point.

Of course you're outside your comfort zone. Law school teaches you:

- an unfamiliar subject,
- in an unfamiliar language,
- in an unfamiliar way.

You will get used to it.

Be patient. It takes time.

FINALLY, anyone who says or acts like they "get it" based on the cases you've read so far is either faking it or having delusions.

Focus on yourself.
Don't think too far ahead.
Take it one assignment, one class, one day at a time.

Everything will be OK. I will be here rooting for you, always.

~Amanda

3.2 Don't worry about cold calls

Please don't stress about cold calls. I did, and I regret it.

Scenes from movies like *The Paper Chase* made law school professors seem like monsters, and before law school started, I played out a dozen scenarios in my mind for what my first cold call could look like.

What a whopping waste of time and energy!

Please don't make the same mistake. Here's some info that I wish I'd known back then. I hope it will help you.

* * *

The cold calls I'm talking about are part of the Socratic Method: rather than explain the reading (as in many college courses), a law school professor typically calls on students and conducts a Q&A.

In the Q&A, you have to respond to questions about the reading and what it means.

Most questions are about a) what happened in a court case you've read and b) what that case means for future situations.

1. Questions about cases include things like:

Who were the parties? What was the theory of liability? Which side won? What did the court hold? Why? Do you agree?

After the first week or so, these kinds of questions will seem routine to you. Just do the reading carefully and know the answers to the basic questions I list about each case. You'll feel fine answering these types of questions.

2. The harder questions involve hypotheticals.

These types of questions ask you to think beyond the reading. What if one fact were different? Would it change the result?

Or imagine a whole new set of mythical facts. Then, knowing what you do about how the first case came out, how do you predict a court would rule on the mythical facts?

The good news today is that:

- Most professors give you some sort of advance notice, such as by designating specific students to be "on call" for certain weeks; and
- Most professors count cold calls 0 percent in your grade.

***

COLD-CALL TIPS

When you get a cold call involving a hypothetical question about a mythical fact pattern:

Do NOT jump to find the "right" answer. The goal is not to know that answer, but to identify the best arguments that can be made for—and then against—that answer.

What could one party say that would sway you to rule their way?

Next, how might the opposing party sway you the other way?

If you think of good arguments to help one side's case, the professor might then call on another student to take the opposing view. Then, there's a sort-of modified debate, where more students may get brought into the conversation.

I know that all of that may seem scary, but I promise you it's infinitely less scary than being called into a partner's office and asked to explain the cases you read right there on the spot. You'll be in front of partners, clients, and judges where you'll need to be able to think on your feet. Use cold calls as an opportunity to learn how to present orally.

And never forget:

Preparing for class = nothing
Preparing for exams = everything

So please don't waste time or energy worrying about cold calls!

3.3 Get ready for a braggart brigade

At the start of law school, there will be braggarts.

They may say they took a comprehensive pre-law prep course and feel "ready to go!"

They may boast they already:

- read the first month's reading,
- met with your professors at office hours, or
- copied all the final doctrinal exams from the library.

They may even proclaim, "I disagree with footnote 29 of the second dissenting opinion" (in the 86-page S. Ct. decision you were assigned to read for class).

Every law school class seems to have a few folks like this. Their behavior can bring down even the most confident new 1L.

These days, people call such folks "gunners." (If it helps, I used to refer to one of our class culprits as "sweater vest, briefcase guy." The image kind of stuck in my mind and ended up helping me to chuckle and block out this noise more generally.)

To be sure, some who are gunning for law review will be perfectly pleasant. Perhaps I was one of them. But when it comes those who pull tricks like I've mentioned above, try this approach:

1. Don't let 'em get to you.

- They usually quiet down after a few weeks, and some can even become great connections. In all likelihood, they only acted obnoxiously because they themselves are not confident.
- No one who is really confident needs to brag about it.
- You need all the positive energy around you to keep imposter syndrome at bay early on, so it's critical to block out all unnecessary sources of stress or insecurity.

2. Don't burn any bridges.

Although your instinct may be to loathe gunners and shun them permanently, DO NOT. Consider every single member of your class to be a future potential colleague, employer, or referral source. Be smart. This isn't high school or college. Exclusionary, cliquey behavior will get you nowhere fast in the legal world.

3. Don't be one of those gunners.

Or at least, be very, very quiet about it. :)

53

3.3 GET READY FOR A BRAGGART BRIGADE

3. Don't be one of those gunners.

Or at least, be very, very quiet about it. :)

3.4 You should "outline" *your* way

"**H**ave you started your outline yet?"

Some gunner with a briefcase asked me that during my very first week. I didn't even know what an "outline" was.

Here's what I wish I knew then:

1. It's not the outline itself that matters. It's the process of creating the outline that prepares you.

YOU must create your outline.

- Do use supplements and commercial outlines, but do so only to clarify your own thinking and enhance your own outline.

2. There is no one "right" or "best" way to outline. There are as many approaches as there are law students.

- You will want to experiment with different approaches to see what works best for you.
- You don't have to abandon what worked for you in school before.

In fact, throughout high school, college, and law school, I did the very same thing:

a. Each weekend, I neatly recopied my daily class notes so I would be able to read and understand them months down the road. The point was to complete professor sentiments that I had scribbled in abbreviated form, fill in any gaps in my notes, delete anything repetitive, and create "final notes" that I could study from and eventually memorize.

b. For each course topic, I consolidated all of my notes from readings and supplements into a single place and made sure they were legible.

c. Then, to outline in law school, I simply married the first two.

My end product was the start of a master document organized by topic, rather than by class date. It ultimately became my "outline" that I whittled down to study for exams.

I hope the above will give you some ideas to create an outline that's right for you.

PS—In my first LinkedIn post about outlining, I asked 2Ls, 3Ls, and JDs to share the approach that worked best for them.

I learned that most do some version of a traditional outline. A typical outline will track and be organized into sections that correspond to the topics in each course syllabus. There are tons of commercial outlines out there that follow the standard format, if you are curious about what traditional outlines look like.

But not all students create typical outlines. Some use flashcards; others use flowcharts; and still others have no outline but only a series of notes and checklists they prepared based on the course materials.

At the end of the day, you need to get all of the information you've learned into your head, so however you decide to accomplish that goal is good.

3.5 Befriend a lonely 1L today

I've seen a bunch of anonymous posts by 1Ls on other platforms that make me so, so sad.

The posts say something to the effect of:

"I haven't found a friend group. Everyone seems to be in their established cliques already. I feel isolated and alone. Any tips?"

I bet you can think of at least one student in the 1L class who might write such a post?

PLEASE give them a friendly smile and say hello today. Better yet, introduce yourself and ask how they're doing.

"Why?" you ask.

Well, if it being "the right thing to do" isn't enough, consider this:

Every single student at your school is YOUR potential:

- colleague
- client
- boss
- referral source, for both future clients and future job opportunities

What if that 1L who's sitting alone in the corner of the cafeteria becomes your client some day? Don't miss this opportunity to make a good first impression.

In fact, I'd say that if you introduce yourself today, you increase the chances of landing that 1L as your client someday.

Don't miss this opportunity.

So be smart. Play the long game.

You may have lockers and daily homework, but this is NOT high school. *Cliques*? That should never be a problem for people during 1L.

Isn't 1L hard enough? Might you befriend a lonely 1L for me today?

CHAPTER 4

MIDTERMS

Dear 1L,

Every year, students stress about their first midterms. Please do not.

How you do on the memo and your final exams DOES matter, and yes, you may have stress with those tasks. Midterms, however, do NOT matter. Please do not waste energy on them except to use them as an exercise to help you.

You simply don't have the mental or psychological bandwidth to waste getting strung out over midterms.

The material in this chapter should underscore this point and also arm you with some information so you know what to expect.

~Amanda

4.1 IRAC exams: what are they?

Most 1L exams (and all bar exams) will start with a hypothetical (hypo, for short) fact pattern, which is typically a chronological recitation of events, or a description of a situation. The idea is for the hypo to resemble the way a client might present actual facts to a lawyer.

After the hypo, the professor typically provides a general "Discuss" prompt or a set of questions that identifies which issues from the hypo you are to discuss. I call these types of law-school exams "IRAC exams," "essay exams," or "issue spotters" (as opposed to exams made up of multiple-choice or short-answer questions).

Your task is to write an essay that:

- identifies the legal **I**ssues arising from the facts,
- states (and explains) the governing legal **R**ule that applies to resolve those issues,
- explains how the legal Rule **A**pplies to the facts in the hypo; and
- predicts which way a court is likely to **C**onclude on the issues.

We use the acronym "IRAC" to stand for the different parts of the essay and the order in which you are supposed to present them, and I refer to these essays as "IRAC essays" in this book.

You will find a selection of my posts with practical tips for handling IRAC essays in Chapter 7.

4.2 Make friends with practice questions

I used to be scared of practice questions. I would read them, have no idea how to answer, and just feel defeated.

Try to look at practice problems as tools to help you rather than "gotcha" questions meant to trip you up.

Reading sample exam questions and answers can really help you understand how legal concepts are applied to new fact patterns.

The best samples are ones from your professor that have model answers. If those are not available to you, use Quimbee, or get answers to hypotheticals from state bar exams. (Many states offer past exams and "best" answers online.)

The *Examples and Explanations* series also has some really good examples—they get you thinking in the way you'll need to for exams.

Try to retype a sample exam answer in your own words. Just copying the words down will help you start to see how courts would apply the legal standards you've learned in new fact situations.

I taught myself a lot of hard concepts, like consideration, this way. Just going to class and taking notes is not enough.

Let me know if you try it and how it works for you.

4.3 What to do if you fail a midterm

When your first and only feedback in law school is a 35/100 on a Contracts midterm, it's time for some serious soul-searching. That was me in October 1993, and I thought the world was going to end.

To be sure, like most all 1L midterms, it was merely a "practice" exam. But to me, it was devastating.

My initial, angry disbelief quickly became embarrassment. I also didn't know what I'd done wrong.

I had done all the reading. I had attended every class. And I had studied SO much.

I knew the material by heart. I really did.

Really!

Some takeaways:

- I failed because the point was to apply the material I knew to brand new situations. I had no idea how to do this. Most 1Ls do not either—in early October.
- You can learn. It just takes practice.
- So, do your soul-searching. Kick and scream; get mad; cry. But get it out of your system and MOVE ON.
- Plan to learn how to write an IRAC essay and start practicing.

A poor midterm grade should not matter. I ended up with a flat A in Contracts. You can, too!

Let's GO!!!

4.4 You learned to swim!

You've been through a lot of challenges in life that were hard.
They tested you.
But you came through.

Remember when you tried to ride a bike for the very first time?
You likely fell.
But you got up, dusted yourself off, practiced, and learned.

Remember when you tried to swim for the very first time?
You likely sank.
But you came up, got your bearings, practiced, and learned.

Now, you're to do 1L for the very first time.

You're likely disoriented.
You feel like you're buried.

But you'll rise up.
You'll practice.
And you'll learn how to do law school, too.

Draw upon the past challenges you've overcome.

You're a highly competent individual.

You learned how to swim. You can learn how to do 1L, too.

4.5 How to beat mid-semester brain fog

It's no wonder that so many law students experience a mid-semester brain fog.

The pace of content for your doctrinal courses seems to be accelerating, and legal writing projects have been taking so much more out of you than anticipated.

Feeling daunted is normal.

But please stop to think about how far you have come.

This time last year, most of you were still waiting to hear back from law schools. An agonizing decision process over where you'd attend came next. Just think about that. It must seem like a lifetime ago.

This year has truly been transformative; what you're doing is extraordinary; and you WILL get through this current fog.

***

PS—Here are a few ideas for how to break brain fog:

1. Sometimes, all that's needed is a switch-up in routine.

Try changing when or where you study or perform other recurring, daily tasks, or switch up how you take notes in class (i.e., if by hand, start typing, and vice versa).

2. Research shows that incorporating a healthy lifestyle that includes mindfulness, exercise, and other restorative activities can significantly improve one's cognitive abilities. So don't ease up on your commitment to these areas.

3. It also always helped me mid-semester to step back and review each course's syllabus; doing so helped me see what we'd covered and where we were going.

The more time you can spend reviewing what you've already learned periodically throughout the semester, the better. Doing that can start to cement some concepts to make them feel less foggy, which should free up your mind to learn new content.

4. Finally, remember to give yourself some grace. What you're trying to accomplish this year is extraordinary. Remember that; pause and reflect; and take a deep breath.

4.6 Class prep is for cowards

You should stop spending so much time preparing for class and start spending more time after class synthesizing what you've learned.

1. Don't worry about cold calls. You should be beyond that by now.

   - Your course grade is the same, whether you answer brilliantly or pass.

2. Skim and book-brief quickly. After class, read answers to sample essay questions. You should start trying to write out answers to practice essay problems.

   - Certainly, start answering practice problems no later than November.
   - Unless you have a very long reading period, you will not

have time in that period to study, outline, and do enough practice problems to ensure that you ace your exams.

3. You will also get VERY busy writing the final memo.

- Last year during final memo preparation, 1Ls found there was a full week or more when they had zero time even to prepare for class (if they attended class at all).
- They had no time to finalize, synthesize, outline, continue to memorize, or do practice problems.

Don't get caught creating your outlines and starting practice tests during reading week.

4. Map out time blocks devoted to outlining and exam prep for the remaining weeks in the semester, skipping the week you're finalizing your memo.

- That way, you won't have to decide what course, or what type of studying, you will do during each time block.

As to what to put in those study blocks, my main message is this: you must pick only highly efficient ways of studying. Preparing for class may give you comfort, but it's highly inefficient.

Being unprepared for class takes courage, but this idea is not new. It is the conventional wisdom everywhere at this point in the semester.

- The approach may cause you short-term unease, but there is no way to do everything. There simply are not enough hours in the day. You need to pick your spots.

- Everything you do should be efficient. Preparing for class is not.

I hear you. I am here for you. I welcome your thoughts and questions. The remaining time in October is precious time that you won't get back. Make every moment count!

Ditch the "which" this Halloween

Dear 1L,

We need to have a little chat about "which" and "that."

You are all using "which" WAY too much.

There's an easy rule and a hard rule. I recommend you follow the easy one for purposes of writing during 1L, even though the hard rule is more accurate.

A: The Easy Rule

Never use "which." Always choose "that."

This rule comes from a memo that Mark Herrmann created for his book, *The Curmudgeon's Guide to Practicing Law*. In the memo, Herrmann lists only ten rules on writing style, and one of them is this:

"[W]hen you have a choice between using the word 'which' and the word 'that,' the word 'that' is correct."

He goes on to note on p.4, "There are exceptions to this rule. Do not worry about them. If you follow my rule, you will be right 95% of the time. If I think that an exception applies, I will make the change." (Herrmann, 2019)

This is a great rule, and I encourage you to adopt it.

Now, if you'd like to learn more and see whether you can handle the hard rule, I offer a silly tale I told about "which" below. You'll see that it requires a three-part analysis.

~Amanda

***

B: The Harder Rule

In the Halloween spirit, I'm dispensing with formal grammar terms and examples you can easily find online. My aim is to try to give you a lesson on "which" that you might remember, even if it's kind of corny.

Rule 1: "Which" sounds like "witch." Witches are bad. So ditch the "which." Use "that."

You'll be right almost all the time.

Now, if you're bent on using "which," and you're really sure you're right, test the "which" under Rule 2.

Rule 2: Test: Get rid of the *entire* "which" clause. Does the sentence still make sense and say what you mean?

If not, use "that."

If yes, the "which" clause can stay, if it absolutely must. But follow Rule 3.

Rule 3: Like a witch needs her broom to take flight, a "which" needs two commas to be right.

Always use two commas around a "which" clause.

Contain that evil witch!

***

PS—If the above is too kitschy for you, below are some formal sources on "which" vs. "that." You can also find many elementary grammar tutorials on the topic.

- Bryan A. Garner, *Garner's Modern English Usage*, at 900-02 (4th ed. 2016).
- Mignon Fogarty, "'Which' versus 'That' - Quick and Dirty Tricks," (Mar. 21, 2008) (grammargirl.com).
- Bryan A. Garner, *The Scribes Journal of Legal Writing* v.13, at 38 (Scribes 2020) (interview with Chief Justice John G. Roberts, Jr.).

NB—Please do not rely on these or any other of my references for proper Bluebook form.

CHAPTER 5

THE MEMO

Dear 1L,

This chapter and the one that follows are really important. They also get very detailed and refer to terms that you won't understand yet.

I anticipate you may want to review them before law school starts so you feel more comfortable going in, but otherwise, you should save these chapters for closer reading in the fall, as they become relevant.

~Amanda

5.1 How to do thorough case-law research

When doing case-law research for a motion or brief, there will come a point in time when you wonder, "Have I done enough?"

Follow these seven steps to make sure you don't miss a key case:

1. Find, pull, and skim three relevant cases (from secondary sources, sample briefs, searches under keywords and headnotes, etc.).

2. Pull and review every case cited within the applicable headnotes of the three cases.

3. If you find new relevant cases, add them to your first three.

4. Repeat steps 2 and 3 on the added cases. Soon, you should start to see the same case names reappearing. Keep repeating steps 2 and 3 on new cases until you're no longer turning up any unfamiliar case names.

5. Shepardize every relevant case you've amassed (filtered by applicable headnote(s)).

6. Repeat the above steps until you are familiar with every case.

7. To be extra, super-duper safe, Shepardize all your relevant cases in whichever of the two databases (WL or Lexis) you didn't use first. (I use WL, but occasionally I pick up another stray case on Lexis.)

There will come a point when:

- you see all the same decisions cited in the cases and Shepard's results;
- no more unfamiliar case names pop up within those cases or results; and
- there are no more cases to Shepardize.

When that point comes, you should have peace of mind (or as much of it as any lawyer ever feels).

It can be a laborious process, this exhaustive-research thing—hence the name, "exhaustive." But you can't be sure you have everything unless you go through each step.

5.2 Avoid a "dicta trap"

Try not to fall into a dicta trap when writing your memo.

It's easy to do.

I did.

It was fatal.

Here's what happened and three lessons learned.

***

A doctor had autopsied the wrong body. It was the corpse of a nine-year-old girl who'd just died. Her mother had given no consent and was undone. The thought of her little girl's body being butchered in that way was just too much for her, and she fell into deep despair.

But dwell on the mother I could not. Instead, under some far-away state's common law, I had to answer: *Was there a viable claim for intentional infliction of emotional distress?*

That was the situation for me in 1993, and I shudder, still, at the ghoulishness of the whole thing, start to finish.

Long story short, I utterly botched the analysis. My mistake was this:

- I focused on what the courts SAID.
- I didn't focus on how the courts RULED.

Essentially, I compared cases by comparing the strength of the language the court used when deciding the issue, rather than comparing a) the facts in my assignment, with b) the facts in the prior court cases that addressed the same legal issues.

It was a trap (a "dicta" trap, I later learned and reference below).

You should focus on these three keys to avoid falling into the same predicament:

1. Don't stray far into what the courts "say."

- Courts say a lot of things called "dicta."
- You don't need to "get" dicta, or where it applies, for the memo. ("Dicta" is short for the Latin phrase, "obiter dictum." It means an "aside," or any statement made by a judge in an opinion that is not necessary to resolve the case before the court, making the statement not legally

binding on other courts.)

- You must focus on the fact patterns and how the courts rule (i.e., which side wins)—not what the courts happen to say along the way.

2. Discuss the cases with FACTS most like yours.

- When you're choosing which cases to use to compare and contrast, pick the cases with the fact patterns most like yours.

3. Compare each case, FACT-to-FACT, with the hypo in your assignment.

You need to get far more specific than you think. Your court's "likely outcome" may turn on details so small as:

- the color a party wore;
- the particular words they used;
- the specific number of trees around their house; or
- the precise number of errors in their work.

As for me, I didn't learn the keys to keep out of the dicta trap until later. Fortunately, a friend relayed them to me. I am forever grateful to her.

5.3 How to organize your cases

After you've completed your research, you've got a lot to do BEFORE you start writing.

The first step is organizing your research and deciding which cases to use in your memo or brief.

Here's how I was trained to do it as a lawyer. I wish I had known how to do it when I was a 1L. In addition to being a time-saving organizational approach, arranging your cases this way can help ensure that you don't fall into a dicta trap.

I hope it will help you generate a system that works for you.

1. I gathered all the cases on an issue and divided them into two piles.

In one, I put the cases that were "good" for my client that I might use affirmatively.

In the other, I put all the "bad" cases that I'd likely need to distinguish.

"Good" meant the court RULED or HELD for a party in a similar situation to my client.

2. At the top of each case, I'd write in colored marker:

- either "good" or "bad"
- the case's procedural posture
- bullets with the key facts that drove the court's outcome
- the date on which I'd Shepardized the case*

The goal was to have written clearly—right on top there—everything that I needed to see to jog my memory on what the case was about and everything important that I'd ultimately make sure I said about the case in the brief I was writing.

That way, I could pick up the case quickly, know what it stood for, and start to see where and how I would use it. It really helped me get a handle on all the cases (which you'll find really do go every which way).

* Adding the Shepardized date is more for practitioners than law students, but it's a really good habit to get into now. It can be a time-saver later for everyone.

5.4 Legal analysis: what is it?

Lawyers on LinkedIn attack law schools for not teaching students the practical skills necessary to be a "real" lawyer. But on one skill, it's the law schools getting it right, and, too often, the "real" lawyers getting it wrong:

The skill is legal analysis.

Consider this four-sentence "legal analysis" from one lawyer's brief in support of a motion for summary judgment:

1. The court should grant D's motion for summary judgment (MSJ).

2. To survive an MSJ...[explanation of legal standard with citations.]

3. P here fails to adduce sufficient proof to survive D's MSJ. See [three cases with parentheticals quoting their holdings].

4. D is thus entitled to summary judgment on P's claims.

That is NOT legal analysis, and the "real" lawyer who wrote it needs to revisit what law schools teach.

To "analyze" means:

    a. to describe the facts of past court cases,

    b. to compare the facts from your case to the facts of those past cases, and

    c. to reason why your case is therefore similar or different from those past cases.

It is only after you have completed all three steps that you're ready to wrap up with a conclusion that the three past cases should persuade your court to rule for your client.

5.5 Budget your time—times ten

Every year, the memo derails some students' semesters because they don't plan ahead.

Legal writing takes a REALLY LONG time. Much, much longer than you expect. And this is your very, very first time writing such a big analysis.

PLEASE budget your time.

Sending you good cheer. I know this is an increasingly intense time, and you are in my thoughts, always.

5.6 Save time with the Flowers Paradigm

Want to get faster at legal writing? Try the Flowers Paradigm.*

Here's the "how-to":

For any writing project, cut your process into four stages. It helps to think of the stages in terms of building a house:

"You can't build a house until you have an idea for what it should look like."

STAGE 1: The Madman. (I call it "The Muse.")

This stage is for brainstorming. You're just supposed to get the ideas down—the good, the bad, and the ugly.

From there, you distill three or four core reasons why one outcome is more likely (in a memo), or why the court should come out your way (in a brief).

Using the house analogy, you might choose the number of floors in the house.

If three, your first, second, and third floors would each be a "core feature," like a "core reason."

You next write out your core reasons in full sentences.

Then you hand off your vision to an architect.

STAGE 2: The Architect.

The architect next must design a blueprint, much like you must make an outline. Without at least a rudimentary one, you'll be lost.

"You wouldn't start building walls to rooms until you know where they will go."

In this stage, you match all your other messy, smaller ideas with whichever core reason they relate to or support.

In the house analogy, you'd decide the number, purpose, and place of the various rooms on each core floor.

Once you've got your blueprint, you pass it to a builder.

STAGE 3: The Builder. ("The Writer.")

The builder next needs to frame out the house, build the rooms, install the drywall, etc.

Here you write sentences to fill out the text of the subreasons, examples, logic, and reasoning.

NB—Before I write, I also cut and paste all the court citations, case briefs, quotes, and other "meat" that I want to use into that section. That way, I'm not writing from scratch.

The house then goes to the painter/editor.

STAGE 4: The Judge. ("The Painter/Editor.")

Your painter now gets to make the house look "pretty" (i.e., revise, edit, cut, cut, cut).

"You wouldn't start applying paint to walls that haven't been built yet."

You shouldn't waste time editing a transition phrase or the style of a sentence only to have it end up in a different part of your brief where the phrase or style doesn't fit.

The key to all three initial stages is not to let your internal editor butt in early.

If you edit yourself when you're trying to think, organize, and draft sentences, you'll only stymie your creativity and stall your ultimate process.

Just get everything down. Worry about how "pretty" it looks later.

(*The above describes the famous framework from English professor Betty Sue Flowers. Bryan A. Garner brought Flowers to the legal writing world. Quoted are sentences that sound like what I recall Garner saying in a lecture on the topic years ago.)

5.7 Your reader wants to hear from *you*

When you're new to legal writing, it's natural to think:

- Courts' words sound better than your words.
- Courts' full sentences should be quoted at length.
- Courts' reasoning will be more persuasive than your own.

Instead, you should know:

- Your words sound just fine.
- Your full sentences are better than long court quotes.
- Your own reasoning will be FAR MORE compelling.

When you write the discussion part of your memo, focus on the facts and outcomes, and put your analysis in your own words. Your reader wants to hear from you!

***

When I wrote my first legal memo, I was positive the courts' reasoning in cases was far more artfully worded and persuasive than anything I could say.

I quoted sentence after sentence of these brilliant judges' words—everywhere I could. My memo was stuffed to the gills with long passages of the cases' well-worded legal prose.

Big mistake.

Here's advice I should have followed. You should, too.

After you've set up your legal standard (where you will often need the exact quoted language from statutes and cases), use YOUR words to write the remainder of your memo.

Paraphrase what the court said and either don't quote at all, or isolate key language to weave short quotes into your own sentences.

EXAMPLE:

Assume you're one of two defendants. You're trying to reduce the damages you must pay if the court rules that you're jointly liable for negligent hiring.

The other defendant argues that comparative fault principles don't apply to negligent hiring claims, just like they don't apply to intentional tort claims. You want the court to reject that argument based on a case you found called "Jefferson."

Don't do this:

The Jefferson court stated, "We conclude that the principles of comparative fault absolutely apply to claims of negligent hiring. We do not hold that comparative fault principles apply to claims involving intentional torts. We have never held such a specious thing." [cite]

Here's how you might paraphrase and use the court's language more selectively and effectively:

The court held that comparative fault principles "absolutely apply" in negligent hiring cases. [cite] The court clarified that it was not holding—and had "never held"—that comparative fault principles applied to intentional tort claims. Id. In fact, the court noted it would be "specious" to do so. Id.

I know you feel nervous using your own words. I did, too. But they're far more persuasive than citing long court quotes, and they'll make your legal writing stronger.

5.8 Six ways to slog through legal-writing fog

No 1L wants to be spending all weekend inside writing a legal memo, but many of you will be.

Please know that even seasoned lawyers get stuck when writing about an area of law they're unfamiliar with. And this is your very first time.

You may get to a point where you think you understand how the analysis works, but the words just won't go from your head to your page.

There's a disconnect between what you *know* and what you can actually explain.

When I got to this point, I'd try one of these approaches.

1. Read briefs.

Pull and read the dispositive briefs from the cases you've assembled to write about. The parties' lawyers were making the same arguments you have to make. Learn from them.

2. Brief the cases you'll use for compare/contrast.

Try typing out a "brief" for each case in a freestanding document. Don't worry about how your writing sounds, but do write in full sentences.

Beyond getting you in the writing groove, putting the cases in your own words—separate and apart from thinking about how they apply to your facts—can really help you understand an analysis more fully.

3. Explain things out loud and transcribe.

Try to explain the legal analysis orally. Pretend you're talking to a ten-year-old. Record yourself and transcribe. Start there for your draft.

4. Revisit your outline.

If you haven't made one yet, please, please try to—at least a high-level one. Doing so should really help you remember what you're trying to establish in each section. An outline is your compass so you don't go off track.

5. Bullet your reasons for your headnote.

Create a bulleted list of reasons you think your client can or cannot show each element of the claim being considered or each factor of the test that applies.

6. Do something else.

Go on a walk, blast music and dance, do push-ups, fold laundry, play basketball, vacuum, mow the lawn, etc. Whatever you do, make it something completely different that gets you out of your head.

Let your subconscious do some of the work. While your brain is not fixating on what you have to write, your brain can make connections that will often surface after you return.

* * *

I hope one or more of these helps you wade through your legal-writing fog faster. I'm thinking of you and cheering you on!!

5.9 The memo is a bear for everyone

Please don't get defeated by how long the memo takes you.

There is nothing "wrong" with you. And it's not just you.

Legal writing just takes a very long time. Remember that you've never done anything like this before. It's all brand new. That makes the legal writing you have to do harder—and even more time consuming—than it usually is.

I know it's a slog.

I hear you and am here for you. I'm sending you extra hours to add in every day.

5.10 Defined terms: two caveats

You need to be careful when you deal with defined terms.

My first point is that you need to be consistent. Once you've defined something, you don't need to—and should not—write it out in long-form later.

Ex. If you've already written, "the school's anti-bullying policy (the 'Policy')," don't later refer to that as "the policy against bullying" or the "school policy." Stick with "the Policy." That avoids reader confusion.

Ex. If you've already defined "The Americans with Disabilities Act" as the "Act," don't later refer to it as the "Disabilities Act," or the "ADA."

The purpose of defining a term is to make clear what you mean when you use the term. Be consistent.

Here's a corollary:

If you're talking about a collision between the motorcycle your plaintiff-client rode and a van that your defendant-opponent drove, do not then refer to either as a "vehicle." Stick with "motorcycle" and "van." (Both are "vehicles," such that referring to either that way says nothing at all about which vehicle.)

Second, you need to be meticulously accurate. Consider this sentence:

"The response to ABC Corp.'s ("ABC") motion is due on __."

Here's the problem with the sentence: It defines "ABC Corp.'s" as "ABC."

That means then every time you write "ABC" again, you need to make sure you are talking about "ABC Corp.'s." as opposed to "ABC Corp." That can't be what you mean.

True, your reader will figure it out, but that's no excuse. As lawyers, we're trusted to be precise, and if you're going to go to all the trouble of defining ABC Corp. as ABC, you should do so accurately.

To define the term accurately, you have two options:

1. Rephrase so that the term is not possessive in the spot where you're defining it.

2. Go ahead and put the apostrophe + s in your parenthetical. If you define "ABC Corp.'s" as "ABC's," it stands to reason that the non-possessive form is "ABC."

Finally, there's a more fundamental question here: Should you even bother to use a definition at all for ABC Corp.?

These days, unless I were discussing another entity in the brief with a similar name, I would not bother: The only reason to define a term is that a definition is needed for clarity, and absent there being an "ABC, Inc." or similar entity in the same case, no reader will be confused if you start referring to ABC Corp. as ABC.

The era of litigators using definitions for everything under the sun in briefs has long passed (at least at the appellate level).

That said, many of your firms may still require defined terms, and at the trial-court level, they seem to be the norm.

But if you are going to bother defining a term, please be precise about it!

Otherwise, your definition may cause your reader added confusion, not added clarity.

5.11 Proofread multiple ways

When you've been intensely working on a big writing project, you get too close to it. You can't see little typos and other nits. You need a freshly rested set of eyes. So try to sleep on it—before you finalize.

Here are some other methods that can help you pick up on things when you proofread:

- Print out a hard copy and proofread from the bottom up.
- Change the font style. Proof in the new font.
- Change the font size, ink color, or line spacing. Proof it in the new format.
- Read your memo aloud.
- Have MS Word read your memo aloud to you.

* * *

I'm sending you all extra energy and better eyes to help you get through. The memo ends up being a bear for most, especially in these final days and hours.

But you WILL get through this!

5.12 Don't flout the formatting rules

Every fall, many 1Ls shoot themselves in the foot when finalizing their memos. They lose a ton of points for no good reason.

The formatting rules from your professor are NOT optional.

Your professor is just like the judge who will read your motions in the future, and all courts—and many individual judges—have detailed formatting rules, too, so you'll want to embrace the rules and not fight them.

When you're a lawyer who gets a new case, one of the first things you do is get your judge's individual rules. You learn them, and you make sure you follow them.

Treat your professor's rules the way you would those of a judge.

A typical set of 1L memo rules says that your memo must be written in 12 pt. font, with one-inch margins, left-justified, and no more than a specific number of pages (e.g., 10–12).

Under this set of rules, do not try to get away with 11.5 pt. font, 0.8 inch margins, or 12.1 pages.

- Your professor WILL notice.
- You WILL lose points.

This is not college. Don't risk breaking the rules.

***

When was the last time you checked your professor's formatting rules for your memo?

Read them again and take note!

5.13 Do your headnotes float?

Before you hand in your memo, check to make sure your centered headings don't float.

If your paragraphs are set to indent 0.5 inches by default, when you "center" your headings, they will NOT be centered. They'll be shifted 0.5 inches to the right.

They'll also be the first thing your professor notices, and they'll cast a huge, sloppy shadow over your whole memo.

Don't lose points over silly things like this. You've got enough else to worry about.

5.14 Sample Memo

As you know, law-school ethics codes prevent anyone from assisting with specific, 1L writing assignments before final drafts are submitted. I see these memos after the fact, when I help students get ready for spring semester and prepare their writing samples for job applications.

Attached at Appendix C is my best representation of what 1L professors are looking for. It is based on what I've seen, what dozens of students have told me during the past few years, and what I've relearned about the way they want you to write during 1L (which differs in a few ways from how litigators typically write in real life).

I have endeavored to prepare a composite style that is largely compatible with all the various acronyms—IRAC/CREAC, etc.—that professors teach.

Caveats:

1. The facts, law, court cases, and quotations in the sample are fictional.

- Please use the sample for illustrative purposes as to structure and writing style only, not for legal doctrine or analysis (it is fiction).

2. In reality, litigators do not often write formal, objective memoranda, and they do so less today than in the past.

- When we conduct a legal analysis, we also usually focus on procedural posture and standard of review. You will focus on those things more in the spring.

3. MOST IMPORTANT: If my model is incompatible in any way with what YOUR specific professor instructs, follow what *your* professor instructs. (This rule goes for everything I say in this book.)

I do think this should get you started, though. I'm sending you all positive energy through this process.

Don't develop a Demi Moore adverb problem

Remember the court scene in *A Few Good Men*?

Tom Cruise says, "I object," and the court overrules.

But Demi Moore isn't satisfied. She just has to get up and say "I strenuously object."

"Strenuously" didn't make the objection any more convincing there, did it? Instead, Demi looked desperate.

OK, she looked like a fool.

Let's avoid that in your legal writing, shall we?

Examples

1. Instead of saying, "The price went up quickly," or "The price fell rapidly,"

Try:

"The price jumped."

"The price surged."

"The price skyrocketed."

"The price plunged."

"The price nosedived."

"The price plummeted."

2. Instead of saying the defendant was "very hungry,"

Try:

"The defendant was famished."

"The defendant was ravenous."

- BONUS: Oomphy words liven your prose, and they take up less space than weak words propped up by modifiers.

Livening prose and saving space in legal writing are always good.

PS—I know you thought adverbs were your friends in college writing. They were an easy way to add to a humdrum verb or adjective. And unless you were writing for an advanced writing class, you likely got away with rampant adverb use.

But as you might have gathered, nothing is "easy" about law school—or legal writing.

- The writing standards have jumped a notch.

So instead of writing *adverb + weak verb*, or *adverb + weak adjective*, try to find stronger, more vivid verbs and adjectives.

PPS—In fact, as you progress down the road of becoming a better writer, I think you'll find that adverbs aren't friends in NON-legal writing, either.

The adverb is not your friend.

Adverbs, like the passive voice, seem to have been created with the timid writer in mind.
—both attributed to Stephen King

Adverbs...are words that modify verbs, adjectives, other adverbs, clauses, and whole sentences, and they're often not very helpful. Usually, they tell us that the writer is in fear of not being sufficiently clear.
—attributed to Anne Lamott

CHAPTER 6

FALL WRITING TIPS

6.1 When to capitalize "court"

You will write the word "court" a lot this year. Get clear now on when to capitalize!

1. CAPITALIZE SCOTUS (Supreme Court of the United States)

Always capitalize "court" when it refers to the US Supreme Court, regardless of where your case is pending.

2. CAPITALIZE YOUR COURT

If your case is pending in the court to which you are writing or referring, you should capitalize that court (absent any contrary, applicable local rule or judicial preference).

Incorrect (although arguably clear): "This court should grant the motion."

It's incorrect because "court" should be capitalized. (You also don't need the "this" before "court"—most of the time.)

Correct: "The Court should grant the motion."

3. IF YOU'RE IN STATE COURT

If your case is pending in a state court, you ALWAYS must capitalize "court" when referring to that state's highest court.

4. DO NOT CAPITALIZE OTHER COURTS

Beyond the above-three situations, do not capitalize "court" unless writing out the full, proper name of that court.

6.2 "Here" and "there" go everywhere

As litigators, we write a lot about how our case compares to past court decisions. So we face the dilemma of how to refer to our case. There are many options, including:

- in this case
- in the present case
- in the instant case
- in the case at bar

All of these options are correct. But I urge you to avoid them in your legal writing—for this year and beyond.

Just write "here."

PS—To be sure, more than "here" is occasionally needed for clarity. Always favor clarity over brevity and style. That said, almost always, a simple "here" will do.

PPS—When it's unambiguous that you're talking about YOUR case, you need no "here" at all.

PPPS—You should refer to the other case as "there."

6.3 A "company" is an "it," not a "they"

In the US, a company is an "it," not a "they."

Do you question what I say?

Here's a primer:

1. A "company" is a collective noun.

Other collective nouns common in legal writing are:

- department
- business
- group
- entity

- Congress
- organization

2. A collective noun takes a SINGULAR verb.

YES: "The company is."
NO: "The company are."

3. A collective noun takes a SINGULAR pronoun.

YES: "The company is famous for its dark chocolate."
NO: "The company is famous for their dark chocolate."

4. The collective-noun designation does not disappear when you are talking about one particular collective noun.

YES: ABC Co. is an "it" that "is." (It is *its* chocolate that's dark.)
NO: ABC Co. is not a "they" that "are." (It is NOT "their" chocolate that's dark.)

***

NB—In British English—and likely in other foreign languages—singular words like "company" can correctly be paired with "they." Don't let such international norms trip you up. In the US today, no company is a "they."

6.4 The comma goes INSIDE the quotes, OK?

In US legal writing, we put a period or comma INSIDE the ending quotation marks, regardless of whether that period or comma appeared in the original, quoted material.

Here are two examples.

NO COMMA IN ORIGINAL

Original: "The complaint lacked sufficient facts to survive summary dismissal, but we grant plaintiff leave to file an amended complaint."

Correct: The court dismissed the complaint because it "lacked sufficient facts," but the court also granted plaintiff leave to file an amended complaint.

- Note that the comma goes INSIDE the ending quotation marks, even though no comma appeared there in the original.

NO PERIOD IN ORIGINAL

Original: "We vacate and remand for further proceedings consistent with this opinion."

Correct: The court "remand[ed] for further proceedings."

- Note that the period goes INSIDE the ending quotation marks, even though no period appeared there in the original.

This may trip up writers because it's done differently elsewhere.*

*Source: Waddington, Anne, *New Hart's Rules, The Oxford Style Guide* (2d ed. 2014).

6.5 Lawyers use two commas
where others don't

You'll write more clearly if you start using the Oxford comma and the TICTAC comma. See legal comma guide in subchapter 6.6.

NB—Some writers only add an Oxford or TICTAC comma if a particular sentence would be unclear without the comma. The problem with that approach is it requires you to stop, think, and wonder to yourself each time: *Is a comma needed for clarity in this particular sentence?*

That's a lot of stopping, thinking, and wondering.

Legal writing takes long enough. Don't make your job harder. Just start using these two commas all the time, and you'll never have to stop, think, or wonder again.

6.6 Legal Comma Guide

1. The Oxford comma

✔ A, B, and C
✘ A, B and C

RULE: DO use a comma before "and" in a list of three or more.

For other types of writing, and in other countries, the style guides vary about comma use. Like me, you might have learned another way. That was not wrong, per se.

- But in US legal English, always use a comma after the B in A, B, and C—always.

2: The TICTAC comma

"TICTAC" stands for "Two Independent Clauses Take A Comma."

✔ A walked, and B ran.
✘ A walked and B ran.

✔ A walked, and she ran.
✔ A walked and ran.
✘ A walked and she ran.

Rule: DO use a comma to link two independent clauses.

- Even if the subject of the 1st and 2nd verbs is the same person ("A" and "she"), you must use a comma.

***

PS—An "independent clause" contains both a subject and a verb and can stand alone as a complete sentence.

6.7 Let's get "i.e." and "e.g." straight, shall we?

I confess, I'm a bit of a Latin geek, but most people aren't, and "i.e." and "e.g." routinely cause mix-ups. In fact, it's one of the top five mistakes Grammar Girl (Mignon Fogarty) says she sees when editing technical documents. (GrammarGirl.com).

Both abbreviations are really common in legal writing, too. You should just learn them now so you don't have to guess or look it up every time. Here's a guide.

A: I.E. = IN OTHER WORDS

"I.e." stands for "id est," which in Latin is "it is," "that is," or "in other words."

You should use "i.e." when you want to provide another way to say something you just said.

- "The student was anxious about the one professor who taught by calling on students at random, i.e., the Socratic method."
- "Before starting law school, John wanted to visit the world's poorest country, i.e., Burundi, to see what conditions were like there."
- "Before approaching the new Whole Foods with her product, she tried the only grocery store in town (i.e., Acme)."

You might also say that the word(s) after the "i.e." should equate to the word or phrase immediately before the "i.e."

B: E.G. = FOR EXAMPLE

"E.g." in Latin means "exempli gratia," or "for the sake of example."

You should use "e.g." after a word or phrase for which you're introducing examples.

- "Professors have different teaching styles, e.g., the lecture method and the Socratic method."
- "John wanted to visit a number of developing countries, e.g., Moldova, Armenia, and Tunisia, before starting law school."
- "Before approaching the new Whole Foods with her product, she tried some other grocery stores (e.g., Acme, ShopRite, Publix)."

Note that sometimes I omit the "and" before the last item in the list. Whether to include is a matter of personal style, and I've seen it done both ways.

C: PUNCTUATION WITH I.E. AND E.G.

1. Periods. The style guides generally endorse including a period after each letter of both abbreviations—and that's how I write them.

2. Commas. A majority of guides also advise using a comma both before and after the abbreviation—which I usually do, too, but have frequently seen done both ways. (Grammar Girl has compiled a handy table of what each style guide says in her blog.)

3. Parentheses. As the above examples show, you may set off an "i.e." or "e.g." phrase with a pair of parentheses, in which case NO COMMA is needed before the abbreviation.

4. Em dashes. At least one style guide (i.e., Merriam-Webster) notes that "i.e." and "e.g." "can sometimes follow" an em dash, and I've seen them used that way.

D: MEMORY DEVICES

For "i.e.," think "in essence." Note that "in" is also the first word in "in other words," the literal translation of "i.e."

For "e.g.," which starts with "e," remember "example." Also, although "e.g." does NOT stand for "example given," if that helps you remember what "e.g." means, then remember it!

6.8 Never forget this "id." rule

You will write the word "id." a lot this year, and it will often be followed by a comma.

"Id." is the way lawyers reference a court case where their preceding reference stated the case's full, proper name. (You may have used "Ibid." this way in your college research papers.) Learn how to write "Id.," and "id.," the right way once, and you'll never need to worry about doing it wrong again:

RULE: The period after the "id" IS underlined. The comma afterwards IS NOT.

✔ <u>Id.</u>,

✘ <u>Id.,</u>

You just need to memorize that.

6.9 How to use the verb "cite"

In lawyer land, we use the verb "cite" to mean "to refer to" or "to reference." Accordingly, there is NEVER a "to" after the word "cite."

We cite cases, we do not cite "to" cases.

[I]t's basically illiterate to put in the to, and it's a shame.

—Scalia, J., cited in Bryan A. Garner, *The Scribes Journal of Legal Writing* v.13, at 52 (Scribes 2020) (interview with Justice Antonin Scalia).

6.10 Avoid common mishaps

Every year, I see the exact same substantive mistakes in 1L legal memos. Here are the biggest culprits:

1. TOO MANY LONG, CONFUSING SENTENCES

Fix: Scan for sentences of two-plus lines. Two lines of standard text contain about 20–25 words. Break apart some long sentences, or pepper in some shorter ones. Your AVERAGE sentence length should be no more than twenty words (and I'd try for less).

- Long sentences are monotonous to read. They also get confusing fast, and they're ripe for comma and pronoun errors.

2. MISSING TICTAC COMMAS

Fix: If a sentence has two independent clauses, you MUST add a comma.

✓ A liked x, and B liked y.
✗ A liked x and B liked y.

- Otherwise, your reader may initially read "A liked x and B" as a complete thought and get tripped up.

3. TOO MUCH PASSIVE VOICE

Fix: Ask yourself "WHO IS ACTING?" for each verb. Put the person (i.e., the subject) coming FIRST in sentences.

✓ Boy hits ball.
✗ Ball is hit by boy.

- Passive sentences kill clarity.
- They're longer.
- They make your reader feel "bleh."

4. ANALYZING NEW FACTS

Fix: Never include a fact in your "discussion" section that you haven't first stated neutrally in your "facts" section. (This is just a legal-writing rule.)

5. MISMATCHED PRONOUNS

Your reader will interpret a pronoun as referring to the closest prior noun of the same number (i.e., singular vs. plural) and the same gender (he vs. she vs. it).

Three questions to avoid over break

Dear 1L,

It's not uncommon to have some dread going into the holiday weekend, especially if you have a big family that likes to ask questions. I wrote the below to try to give the heads-up to some of those nosy family members, but I hope it will also make YOU feel better. The truth is, it is exceedingly rare for a 1L to know what they plan to do with their law degree. Please don't feel like you have to apologize for that!

~Amanda

To whom it may concern—

If you plan to see any law students this weekend, here's a list of questions you should NOT ask them:

1. What kind of lawyer are you going to be?
2. Where will you be working this summer?
3. Where will you be working after law school?

For 1Ls, they likely have absolutely no idea.

Your questions will surely cause great stress. They will remind 1Ls that they actually need to be applying for summer jobs now, or soon (traditionally, most jobs have application deadlines sometime in January). 1Ls cannot take any unnecessary stress right now. They have exams right after the holiday. Please do not add to their stress.

For 2Ls, many will also have no idea.

They may know what they'd like to do in an ideal world, but law students often have less power over choosing their initial jobs than one might think. The stakes are even higher for 2Ls, too, because they are farther along, which will increase the stress your questions cause.

For 3Ls, if they don't have a job lined up yet, these questions will mean MAXIMUM stress.

You wouldn't ask a jobless person these questions. Please don't risk it with a law student. (But if you are in a position to help get them a job, PLEASE OFFER to help!)

CHAPTER 7

DOCTRINAL EXAMS

Dear 1L,

This chapter is all about how to write the essay exams for issue spotters in doctrinal classes. At times, I will reference substantive topics in my examples, and I may use words and phrases that are foreign to you. Please don't let that cause you stress. You will learn all about everything substantive during your law school classes.

That said, the sooner you start to familiarize yourself with these new concepts, the more comfortable you will feel when you encounter them for real.

You may also find that some of what I write about exams repeats itself in more than one section in this chapter. That's partly a function of how I wrote the content underlying this book, but any tips I repeat should be telling: it means they are critically important, and I want you to start incorporating them into your own brain and remembering them.

If you are reading this book before you start law school, here's the MOST important thing I want you to take away from this chapter:

Come back to it and read it again before exams!! At that time, everything should make more sense, and I hope you'll have some real "aha" moments.

~Amanda

7.1 IRAC exams: what are they, again?

Recap:

"IRAC exams" (also called "issue spotters" and "essay exams") give you a hypothetical fact pattern followed by a "Discuss" prompt or a set of targeted questions to answer based on the fact pattern.

You should use an IRAC or CREAC framework for your answers, as your specific professor has instructed. It is always the "A" section where you'll want to focus your time and attention.

Following is a little rant I posted on the topic of essay exams, followed by some introductory tips.

* * *

I've never understood why law schools don't have a course designed to teach students HOW to write the essays that professors expect you to produce on final exams.

You've got doctrinal classes; they teach you:

- how to understand legal rules and cases; and
- how to present both sides of an issue ORALLY.

You've got research and writing classes; they teach you:

- how to use cases and citations;
- how to structure and write an office MEMO; and
- how to present both sides of an issue in that office MEMO.

But on your final exams, you get tested on:

- how to structure an exam ESSAY; and
- how to analyze both sides of an issue IN WRITING.

So here's my question:

WHY ISN'T THERE A LAW SCHOOL COURSE ON IRAC EXAMS???

OK, rant over.

In the pages that follow, I'm going to try to teach you a little of what the nonexistent "exam class" should have taught.

Here are some initial pointers I want to make sure you're clear about.

1. What to do if the question is NOT an "issue spotter."

For an exam where your professor gives you a specific question that identifies the issue and its parties:

a. Don't discuss other, unrelated issues or parties.
b. Make sure your answer focuses only on the specific question asked.

2. Don't assume there is a "right" outcome for any issue.

Often, professors will use hypotheticals that could go either way (just like in your legal writing class, where some of your classmates came out different from you in the memo).

3. Getting the "right" answer is worth only a small fraction of points.

Even on questions that do have a right (or better) answer, it's not enough for you to reach that right answer. Instead, you must present the best, most logical arguments for both sides and explain why one side's arguments are more persuasive than the other's.

7.2 How a case proceeds in the real world

I realize that you have a laser focus on exams, but learning about the order of things in the real world can serve as a useful framework for writing an exam essay.

Here's how things work in a civil case:

The plaintiff (P) files an initial pleading with the court called the complaint. In it, P asserts facts and legal claims (a.k.a. causes of action), which are the legal theories under which P is suing the defendant (D) in the lawsuit.

- Examples of claims you learn are a) negligence and b) breach of contract.

On each of the claims, P has the burden of proof. That means the onus is on P to establish each of the claims. The D need not disprove the claims.

Often there are elements P must show to state and ultimately prove to prevail on a claim. Other times, there are factors the decision-maker will consider when evaluating whether P can prevail.

For example, the elements of a Claim of Battery are:

a. a volitional act by D

b. that D intended to cause contact with P,

c. that is harmful or offensive, and

d. that causes P to suffer a contact that is harmful or offensive.**

**NB—Please modify elements to match your professor's wording in class.

P bears the burden of proving every element of every claim.

Next, unless it seeks to admit liability, D raises defenses by which it can try to prevent P from meeting the burden of proof on each claim element.

D does not bear the burden of disproving any of the elements. D just wants to prevent P from establishing the elements. Stated another way, D tries to show that P has not met the burden of proving the elements.

Think of the defensive arguments as the flip side of the elements. So if P says D acted below the standard of care, D will argue that it acted within the standard of care.

- Every element is a potential bone of contention. Every element needs its own IRAC on any exam (although some may be conceded, or obvious and short to discuss).

It is only by knowing the conclusions on each element that you can judge whether P has likely made the claim.

- You arrive at your conclusion on the claim by knowing whether all of its elements are met.

Finally, make sure you're clear on the difference between "Defensive Arguments" and "Affirmative Defenses."

DEFENSIVE ARGUMENTS

Defensive arguments seek to prevent the P from meeting her burden of proof with respect to the elements of a claim.

The D's defenses should support a conclusion opposite from that which the P seeks with respect to each element.

The D does not bear the burden of disproving the elements of a plaintiff's claim.

Discuss defenses and claim elements within the same section under each element, presenting the positions of both P and D, with adequate weight on each.

AFFIRMATIVE DEFENSES

Affirmative defenses are analytically distinct from regular defenses. (Another name for affirmative defenses in Torts is "privileges").

- Some of the affirmative defenses that you'll learn are self-defense, assumption of the risk, and comparative and contributory negligence (Torts); and mistake, incompetence, and illegality (Contracts).

With affirmative defenses, D seeks to avoid or limit liability or damages EVEN IF the P is successful in proving all the elements of a claim.

- The most common example is a criminal case where the D admits to carrying out a crime, but argues insanity to try to get off the hook.

Key for your purposes are two things:

- You must discuss affirmative defenses separately from your discussion of the elements of a claim. Never jumble.
- Do a full IRAC for each element of each applicable affirmative defense. Remember to give attention to both the D's position and the P's position.

NB—The above focuses primarily on courses like Torts and Contracts, where the issues involve the merits of a claim. Civ Pro differs terminology-wise, because procedural rules, not the merits of a claim, are the focus, but the underlying structure of a Civ Pro essay is the same as in other courses.

7.3 Try wearing two hats in every exam

My secret to law-school exams was wearing two hats.

I wore them in all three bar exams I took, too.

One hat was pink, pale pink;
the other blue, denim blue.
And no, I was not going cuckoo.

Each hat had a letter on it—P in pink for the plaintiff, and D for
the defendant in blue.

I assigned each character in the hypo as P or D, and then I started
my quick-change act:

FIRST, I put on my P hat and read the fact pattern.

I played P's lawyer and looked for clues:

- how can I sue?
- which facts will help me?
- what are my strongest points to win against blue?

I brainstormed possible claims, made lists of relevant facts under each one, and came up with a plan.

I then quickly scribbled it down in a rudimentary outline. I did it the old-fashioned way, just pad and pen.

SECOND, I removed the pink hat—quite abruptly, as I had to move fast.

I then donned the blue cap and started again.

I was now on team D, and I had my work cut out to do.

- how can I defend against P's claims?
- which facts will help me?
- what affirmative defenses must I prove?
- and, of course, do I have a chance to counter sue?

I scribbled down D's lists and forged a different plan.

THIRD, it was off with the hats, just me again.

It was time to recall case law and policies to fill into my penned outlines. Deep into my memory book I would go.

FINALLY came writing time.

I had to do it swiftly.

I had to make ALL the best points for each side.

I couldn't be sure who would win on any claim, after all.

BUT having been through my hat acts, I had a big, fat clue.

I simply asked myself,

- which side's case was easier for me to do?

Usually, it was in my gut and I knew.

I made an educated guess at the final conclusion, added a "because," and explained which side had the stronger case and why.

***

And so, dear 1L, I wonder: Might my hats help you?

And yes, I mean all of the above figuratively. But wow, wouldn't that be something if someone actually did this literally?!

7.4 Who should win this driveway caper?

I wrote this story to illustrate how to think about the hypotheticals you'll see on exams. It is 100 percent fiction.

***

We have a narrow driveway that abuts our garage. Only one car fits at a time. Backing out takes care. You really have to keep the car perfectly straight, or you'll sideswipe the garage. It's a pretty short driveway, though, and it's straight, so you wouldn't think of it as a likely accident scene.

Yet one summer Saturday, early in the afternoon, Daughter 1 took "her" car to go to a friend's. Late afternoon, Daughter 2 borrowed Dad's car to go grocery shopping.

So, I am told, somehow…as Daughter 1 (returning from her friend's) was pulling in, Daughter 2 was backing out (to go do errands).

All I know is that two cars collided. (No one was hurt; it was minor; but we own both cars and have high deductibles, so it is doubly unfortunate.)

In any event, I heard it happen from the kitchen. As I came out to see, they were yelling at each other (of course).

D1: You just rammed the back of the car into me!
D2: No, YOU hit *me*. I was backing out. You plowed ahead into me!
D1: …[you get the gist].

It went back and forth. It was a caustic listen, but I let them go at it for a while, for I was actually learning a lot of key facts. D1 was on the phone. D2's music was blasting. D1 wasn't wearing her glasses. The setting sun shone at D2's eye level. D1 rounded the corner "coming in hot."

Eventually, I threw up my hands and told them to stop. I have no clue who was more in the wrong. But I can decide that both, or neither, were to blame, and remind them (sternly) never to drive doing any of the things they were doing.

If I were a judge or jury deciding their dispute, though, I would have to hear both out and reach a conclusion.

The "A" part of an IRAC essay could be like this.

Substitute the names in your hypo for D1 and D2 (you can call them P and D). Have their argument on the driveway. Visualize them making their best "case." Write it all down. It would look like this:

"P claims D was not keeping a proper lookout because she was on her phone. D says it was P who breached the duty of care by driving distracted and too fast—based on the music blasting and her rounding the corner at warp speed. P says D couldn't see because she didn't have her glasses on and the sun was in her eyes. [Mom] decides in favor of [P/D] because __ ."

That is how the "A" part proceeds. The back-and-forth is the factual "Analysis." Mom's decision is the "Conclusion."

Be creative. Make sure both sides get a full airing. Make all reasonably plausible arguments. (Stop when any more would just make your face blush.)

You can always go back and polish how it is written, if you have time, but you will have captured all the rubric fact points. After those are exhausted, have the Ds argue any applicable policy or court case(s) for their sides, or you can do policy/cases after the "because __" for the conclusion piece.

7.5 Create an exam ritual

As your very first law-school exams draw near, you'll want to think about planning your test-taking approach now, so you don't freeze up on exam day or spend too much time on any one question.

Here's the approach that I found worked best.

First, I got a bird's-eye view of the exam as a whole and calculated how much time each question was worth.

Second, I scanned the questions to get a sense of their topics.

Third, I evaluated which question I thought would be easiest for me to attack first.

This three-step approach gave me a set routine—something non-difficult to do—for right when I opened the exam.

It helped to stave off the nerves I'd get right when a test started, and it ensured I spent the appropriate time on each question.

By focusing on and completing the easiest question first, I also got in the writing groove and gained confidence and calmness for the remaining, harder questions.

7.6 Try this last-minute shortcut

I wanted to share a shortcut that helped me learn, memorize, and save time during the final hours before an exam. I hope it can help you.

Sometimes, when a final (or bar) exam was just days away, I was still trying to (re-)master a lot of concepts and then memorize rules. I just didn't have it in me to take practice tests. So I didn't try.

I just read a lot of model essay answers. I hardly looked at the hypos. I just read the answers passively.

Seeing how essays were written on hard topics brought things into focus. Often, on exam day, I would remember a sample essay and be able to regurgitate it. Stories from model answers "stuck" more in my head than lists of rules.

I would write the model that was fresh in mind, plugging in the facts from my own exam hypo, plus any cases stressed in class.

If you read enough answer essays, you start to see patterns. You also have models in your head for how certain analyses might go.

Reading passively takes a lot less brainpower than cramming rules into your head or taking practice exams. It was productive when my brain was too spent to "study" more at night.

I thought you might try it. I will try to think of anything else to recommend. I am thinking of you and hope you are hanging in OK!

PS—Reading sample exam questions and answers can really help you understand how legal concepts are applied to new fact patterns. Most students use Quimbee. The *Examples and Explanations* series also has some really good examples—they get you thinking in the way you'll need to for exams.

PPS—Try to retype a sample exam answer in your own words. Just copying the words down will help you start to see how courts would apply the legal standards you've learned in new-fact situations. (I taught myself a lot of hard concepts, like consideration, this way. Just going to class and taking notes is not enough.)

7.7 Should you pre-write your rule statements?

I've read about law students pre-writing their "rule statements" for use in their essay answers.

In other words, they pre-type paragraphs that state and explain each possible rule, and then on an exam question giving rise to the rule, they simply plop in the pre-prepared "R" part of their IRAC essay.

I'd never heard of doing this (we handwrote our exams), and I'm not sure how it would work logistically—perhaps it's only an option for take-home exams—but I wanted to get your input.

Have you tried pre-writing rule statements, and if so, was it helpful? I see pros and cons.

It certainly might save you time when typing answers on an exam, and it would help ensure a complete rule statement.

On the other hand, for most rules, there will be more potential explanation sentences than apply to any specific exam hypo. For those, you'd need to be meticulous about omitting the irrelevant explanations from your answer.

Overall, I lean toward the view that as long as you tailor template rule statements to fit specific questions, there's no real downside to pre-writing.

Even if you don't end up using your pre-writes, the exercise of typing up all the rules and explanations in your words should help cement them in your mind.

7.8 Most 1Ls start issue-spotters the wrong way

Most 1Ls do this:

- read the question;
- try to figure out the answer; and
- then write an essay to justify that answer.

Instead, do this:

- read the question;
- write one side's best arguments;
- write the other side's best arguments; and
- explain why one side has the better arguments.

It is only AFTER you have explained why one side's arguments are better that you should reach a conclusion in your mind. Making this one change in mindset can be the difference between an A and a B.

7.9 Eight bullets for better exam essays

1. Brainstorm and outline first.

If I could give you one piece of advice, it would be to stop, think, and outline your answer before you write a single word. In addition to promoting a more polished and well-reasoned final essay from you, outlining first ensures that you proceed deliberately, so you don't miss out on any issues and lose free points.

- If I had allotted one hour for a question, I'd typically spend at least 15 minutes thinking about, planning, and organizing my essay before starting to write. The more disciplined you can be about this pre-writing work, the more organized and thorough your final product will be.

2. Consider both sides of every issue before reaching a conclusion.

This means that for each element of a legal issue, you should present all logical arguments for each side. Don't jump to what you think the ultimate outcome will be. You need to include all logical arguments for each side in your essay.

Sometimes, one or more elements of a legal issue will be so one-sided from the hypo that there are no logical arguments for one side.

- You'll end up discussing those elements only briefly in your final essay, if at all, but unless you go through the thought process and ask yourself what logical arguments each side has for each element or factor, you risk overlooking something your professor expects you to discuss.

3. Work the problem.

Don't rush to try to figure out the conclusion to an essay question. You need to "work the problem" first.

When you're brainstorming and outlining before you start writing, go through each claim element (or legal-test factor) one by one; consider all hypo facts that favor each side BEFORE reaching any conclusions about anything.

- Use this approach even if your professor wants CREAC. Simply insert your conclusion at the start of the essay at the end, AFTER you've worked the problem.

4. Show your work.

This means that after you go through the messy pre-writing process, you can't just leave all that hard work on the cutting-room floor.

Make it sound "pretty" and put this work into your final product—EVEN WHEN you know you're presenting arguments that favor the losing side.

5. Rely heavily on the word "because."

When making any legal conclusion, always add a "because" clause, or some other cause-and-effect wording. You need to explain the WHY behind all of your conclusions.

E.g., instead of writing, "A court would likely conclude there was a valid offer," write, "A court would likely conclude there was a valid offer because __ [insert reasoning based on relevant facts, cases, or policies]."

- And don't worry about being too repetitive using the word "because" in your essays. "Because" is a special word in legal writing that does not tire easily, even when used repeatedly.

If you want style variation, try: "A court would likely reach its conclusion in favor of P/D for # reasons. First,... Second,... etc."

6. Remember your professor.

You are not just taking Torts, Contracts, Evidence, Con Law, or whatever your courses may be called. Instead, you are taking each respective course WITH a very certain Prof. __.

That means that an "A" essay in YOUR course will not include all the same ingredients as an "A" essay in someone else's course that happens to be called the same thing. Use the examples, cases, and rule wording that YOUR professor used in class, not those of some hornbook writer.

7. Ask yourself if there's a public policy that helps either side.

Many law students get good at using the facts and case law in their essays, but they leave points on the table by forgetting to consider public policy. So when brainstorming arguments that favor each side, remember to ask yourself if any policy could help one side or the other.

8. Ask yourself if there's a minority view.

As much as students forget to discuss public policies, they forget to mention when the courts in a minority of states would rule "the other way." Minority views come up most often in Torts, if memory serves, but you should make an advance list of all sub-issues that involve minority viewpoints, so if you get a question on that sub-issue, you'll remember to mention it.

7.10 Nine steps to outline an exam essay

This chapter sets forth the steps to take when outlining your answer essays and represents a parallel to the template that comes up next.

***

Follow these nine steps to make sure you don't miss out on points in your IRAC essay.

1. Identify the BIG ISSUES.

Isolate each relevant claim and affirmative defense as a Big Issue.

- A CLAIM is a cause of action like battery, breach of contract, burglary, etc. Label the person asserting a claim as plaintiff (P).
- An AFFIRMATIVE DEFENSE (AD) is a theory by which a defendant (D) may escape liability/culpability even if P would otherwise make a claim. Lack of personal jurisdiction and contributory negligence are examples. Label the person asserting an AD as defendant (D).

2. State and explain the RULE for Big Issue 1.

Starting with Claim 1, recite each of its elements (i.e., what P must prove to make the claim, or what factors the court relies on to decide if P can prove such a claim).

For today, assume Claim 1 has three elements, A, B, C: "To state Claim 1, P must show A, B, and C."

3. Identify the SUB-ISSUES

Take each element (or factor) separately, one at a time, as its own sub-issue.

E.g., "The (Sub-)Issue is whether P can show Element A."

(If your professor prefers a conclusion up front, leave that blank for now, but remember to fill in at the end.)

4. State and explain the RULE for Element A.

Write, "To show A, a plaintiff must __."

5. APPLICATION for Element A.

(a) Make P's case for why she shows A, using arguments based on facts, logic, case law, and/or public policy ("flc&p");

—AND—

(b) Make D's case for why P does NOT show A, using arguments based on flc&p.

6. State CONCLUSION on Element A.

Predict how a court would come out on Element A, explaining the key factors that would sway the decision (and fill it in at the top if professor prefers).

"As to Element A, a court would likely side with [P or D] because __."

7. Repeat steps 1–6 for every other Element (B, C, etc.).

8. State your CONCLUSION on Claim 1.

Predict how a court would decide Claim 1 based on your conclusion for Elements A, B, and C.

9. Repeat steps 1–8 for every AD to Claim 1.

***

Get likely bonus points for:

- stating how a minority jurisdiction would come out and why;
- using specific examples that prof used in class; and
- stating how a change in one or more facts could change the outcome.

7.11 IRAC {CREAC} Essay Template

Dear 1L,

I've been working really hard on something for you. It's a template for an IRAC essay showing my mental process for going about exams and how I outlined my analysis of each issue—BEFORE I wrote a single word.

- I used this same framework for every course and topic—not just in law school, but on successful bar exams for three states.
- And last year, one of my students used it for all his essays and got straight As!

Try using it for practice problems and see what you find. I really think it will help you.

***

I'm thinking of you every day and sending you serious studying mojo!

~Amanda

IRAC {CREAC} ESSAY TEMPLATE

ISSUE: Should the plaintiff (P) prevail on the claim? {Conclusion: P should/should not prevail on the claim.}

RULE: To prevail on the claim, P must show Elements A, B, and/or C. [Or P must win a totality of Factors A, B, and/or C, or P must show [describe].] {Explanation: *[Briefly describe the claim or rule generally as it relates to the question.]*}

APPLICATION: *[Do a baby IRAC for each element/factor.]*

Element/Factor A:

I: The first sub-issue is whether P can show A.

R: To show A, P must show ____ *[explain what it means to show A].*

A: 1—P CAN show A because: *[make P's case on A with facts, logic, cases, policies (flcp)].*

2—P CANNOT show A because: *[make D's responding arguments on A, with flcp].*

3—P CAN show A because: *[Make P's reply points (if any) to what D argued].*

C: P probably **can/cannot** show A **because**: *[summarize key reasons].*

Element/Factor B:

I: The second sub-issue is whether P can show B.

R: To show B, P must ____ *[explain].*

A: 1—P can show B because: *[Make P's case on B w/ flcp].*

2—P CANNOT show B because: *[Make D's responding arguments on B w/ flcp].*

3—P can show B because: *[Make P's reply arguments (if any) to what D argued].*

C: P probably **can/cannot** show B **because**: *[summarize key reasons].*

Element/Factor C:

I: The third sub-issue is whether P can show C.

R: To show C, P must ___ *[explain].*

A: 1—P can show C because: *[Make P's case on C w/ flcp].*

2—P CANNOT show C because: *[Make D's responding arguments on C w/ flcp].*

3—P can show C because: *[Make P's reply arguments (if any) to what D argued].*

C: P probably **can/cannot** show C **because**: *[summarize key reasons].*

CONCLUSION: P **should/should** not win on Claim 1 **because** P can/cannot show A, B, and/or C.

Earn potential bonus points for:

- using specific examples discussed in class;
- saying how an issue would come out if in a minority jurisdiction;
- saying how an issue would come out if a fact or facts changed.

AFFIRMATIVE DEFENSE?

Do a full, separate IRAC {or CREAC} where the D bears the burden of proof on the affirmative defense and goes first, with the P making the responding arguments and the D making arguments (if any) on reply.

Introduction to 1L summer jobs

Dear 1L,

Hi, and happy holiday week! It's been a minute since we talked. I hope you've settled in at home and have had some much-deserved sleep and TLC. I hope you know how proud I am of you for making it through the fall.

Whenever you're ready to gear up and think about law school again, I've collected some information for you about the upcoming 1L and 2L summer-job-search process.

1. Typical 1L summer jobs these days include:

- working for a state court judge (federal court for the very lucky);
- being a research assistant for a law-school professor or for the law-school research librarians; or
- being a legal intern at some other private or governmental entity.

2. Recruiting for BigLaw jobs starts even EARLIER than last year:

- At some top schools, the big firms started holding recruiting events and talking to 1Ls in October this year, and they have job fairs, dinners, and other events starting this winter.
- Big firms are also increasingly starting 1L associate programs to get ahead of recruiting for jobs after 2L and 3L; many more firms also have big diversity-scholarship programs for 1L associates.
- Official OCI is in July, with many firms and schools participating in a pre-OCI right after 1L exams are through this spring.

3. Where to find 1L summer job listings:

Your law school's career-placement office will be best to advise you on where to find listings, but please don't limit yourself.

- An excellent book that shows you how to get lots of additional sources for job listings is Brian Potts's *The Jobless Lawyer's Handbook*. It's short, and it's written in a fun style to read.
- I hope you'll pick up a copy for yourself, but the entire

thing has also generously been made available by PDF on LinkedIn.

4. Goals for any 1L summer job:

Finally, keep in mind these four goals that most try to accomplish in any 1L summer job:

a. Accumulate relevant and interesting experiences to talk about during interviews for 2L summer jobs.

b. Explore areas of law or ways to practice law. By learning about how different types of lawyers spend their days, you will help hone your thinking on what you want to do with your JD.

c. Make contacts in the legal industry that can write recommendations for you and help you with your career.

d. Gain practical legal skills not available in law school.

***

I'll look forward to chatting soon.

~Amanda

March 2024

PART III: 1L SPRING

CHAPTER 8

JANUARY JUMP-START

8.1 Gain perspective on fall grades

Hi. I hope you are OK. Everyone seems to be in some state of reeling right now, with fall grades coming in.

If you didn't get what you'd hoped for, please know there's nothing wrong with you, and you are not some sort of screwup.

- What happened is you got screwed by a brutal curve.

I do not fully understand why law schools grade this way, or why the curve at one law school can be so dramatically different from that at another. But those debates are for another day.

Right now is a time for frustration, and also some shock, for sure. But you know and I know you are an excellent student. You got into law school because of good grades. The problem is that so did everyone else.

There is a RAZOR THIN distinction between one grade and the one above it, and also the one below.

So it's OK to be disillusioned and feel a bit taken aback by your transcript. Ninety percent of you will be.

But:

When you are ready to come out of the funk, here is some GOOD NEWS:

1. First semester grades reflect nothing about how excellent a lawyer you will be. You have the ability to become an excellent lawyer if you choose.

- Focus on getting the training you need to become that excellent lawyer.

2, True, it's nice to get good grades; they smooth short-term paths. But at the end of the day, it's what you choose to do now— AFTER those grades—that will define your future path.

- Don't wait another day to get started.

3. You are learning to become a lawyer, and you will. But everyone has to learn the exam-taking skill at their own pace.

Want to speed up the process? You just need to prioritize things a bit differently and practice more. It is more within your control than it seems.

- I'll have more resources coming up to help you with a strong start to this semester.

That said, back to the moment.

First semester grades were not what you hoped for. Get mad. Yell. Hate the system. But do it quickly. And then,

GET ON WITH IT.

Let's move on like gangbusters into the spring!

I am cheering for you from the sidelines—always.

8.2 Learn the law-school curve

I was shocked when I learned how widely the grading curves vary among US law schools.

- A handful of top schools are entirely pass/fail, and at the T14s I'm aware of, no one really gets below a B.
- Yet at many other schools, a large percentage of students fail or lose scholarships after 1L fall. The "average" is a B- or even a C.
- The remaining bucket of schools fall somewhere in between.

How does one make sense of it all? And how do you know how to feel when evaluating your own grades? That's tough, and I'm wrapping my arms around you from afar.

8.3 Take inspiration from Justice Kagan

Supreme Court Justice Elena Kagan reportedly got her lowest law-school grades during 1L fall. True, she was at Harvard, but her B and B- grades from her first fall were not something she raced to "write home about."

Her story should inspire you.

Why?

She turned things around in the spring, earning three flat As and one A-.

She then:

- became a supervising editor on law review,
- graduated magna cum laude,
- clerked for Supreme Court Justice Thurgood Marshall,
- became dean of Harvard Law School and US Solicitor General, and
- eventually took her own seat on the high Court.

You can't all be Elena Kagan, but you CAN turn things around.

I'll have ideas for you on how to do that, coming up.

8.4 How to boost spring grades

I wish I had a magic potion. You all could take it and convert Bs, Cs, and Ds into As this spring. But alas, I have only my words. So please listen:

If you want your spring grades to differ from those of the fall, YOU must do something different. It's not enough to study "longer" or "harder" this semester. You need to study "smarter." And if you're doubting that a change in habits or study tactics is needed, consider these words commonly misattributed to Einstein:

Insanity is doing the same thing over and over again and expecting different results.

Aside: I question whether "insanity" is really appropriate. It seems more like common human nature to keep plugging away at something until we "get" it. But the premise is still valid—especially when time is so short. So here are some recommendations for change:

- Read immediately before class, preferably in the time block right before class, as often as your class schedule permits.
- Stop reading word for word before class. Skim for the skeleton only.
- Perform tasks requiring brain cells as early in the day as possible.
  - Use the time before your first morning class. It is precious.
  - Use the time between classes. It is precious, too.
- Sleep eight hours every day—preferably during the same time periods each day.
- Include a daily time block for restorative activities. (Exercise works wonders.)
- Take off 24 consecutive hours each weekend (unless your brief is due).

To be sure, adopting the above means you will NOT be 100 percent prepared for class. That's OK. Remember:

Being prepared for class = nothing.
Being prepared for exams = everything.

8.5 Banish January blues

These days, it's easy to get blue.

It's another winter Sunday,
In the library, you will be.
School's the lone social outpost.
Your desk is where you are most.
It's all work, no play.
Grind, grind, grind away.

Please know that I'm thinking of you. I don't have any magic remedy, but here are some things I've been doing for myself this winter to try to feel better (and to stay more cheerful) during the cold, dark days in Pennsylvania:

Exercising outdoors (which, for me, means walking), on as many days as winter permits. —I'm really trying to stick to it this year, too.

Adding brighter lights to my workspace
—I have special "happy lamps" for seasonal affective disorder, but even just switching to brighter light bulbs in regular lamps can perk up a room. You might try.

Surrounding my workspace with cheerful, colorful images.
[Photo omitted.]

8.6 You don't need politics for Con Law

At my law school, there were two camps when it came to Con Law.

In one were the PoliSci/Gov. majors. And their friends, the read-multiple-newspapers-every-day types.

They assembled in the library lounge to read the library's hard-copy subscriptions each afternoon. And they blathered on about politics.

In the other camp were people like me. We had no relevant major. East Asian Studies/Japanese would not help me now. I also didn't read a newspaper every day (despite my father's longtime pleas). I read *Cosmo*. Maybe *Tennis Magazine*.

Worse still, in class, our professor talked ONLY about politics. I didn't know the players. I had never heard of most issues.

It's sort of embarrassing, in retrospect. But I was just a kid of 23. Sure, I was responsible and smart. I did well in school. But fun, for me, was NOT reading the newspaper.

What saved me? The Constitution.

I kid you not.

Read it. It is short.
Type it. Every word. Type every Amendment, too.

As you know, there are three branches of law makers—each with different powers that are overlapping, checking, and interfering. There are lots of moving parts.

It's so much easier to get a handle on where the powers rest—which branch can do which things—when you can visualize the moving parts. You need to really see them in your mind, or on the page, to keep track of things.

But to be able to do so, you need to make the text of the Consti-tution "your own."

You need to know it, cold. Back and forth.
Inside and out.

This task is not onerous.

The Constitution is surprisingly short.

You can highlight and circle. You can have different font colors.
The Constitution shouldn't be some big, scary document.

Make it your own.

* * *

You don't need to know politics.
Know the Constitution.

The Constitution saved me.
The other camp?

Not so much.

CHAPTER 9

THE BRIEF

9.1 Summary judgment primer and sample sentences

Many of you are writing summary judgment briefs under Rule 56 this spring. Yet in your fall Civ Pro class, you're lucky if Rule 56 even came up. Worse still, you've never written a summary judgment brief before.

I thought a little primer on the process we use for this type of motion in the real world would help you feel like you have a better handle on things. See Part 1.

At the end are some model sentences you can steal for your own briefs. See Part 2.

PART I:

To begin, plaintiff (P) files a complaint in federal district court. She serves a summons on defendant (D). There may be a motion to dismiss or other early things, but eventually, D answers the complaint.

The next step is discovery.

The parties exchange written questions that seek information, along with requests for production of documents, inspections, and other things.

The parties then exchange answers and responses, etc. Depositions and other things happen, and ultimately, discovery closes.

There is now an evidentiary record.

At this point, either party may move for summary judgment under Rule 56.

The goal of a brief in support of a motion for summary judgment (MSJ) is to persuade the court to rule on a claim as a matter of law.

The theory is that no dispute of material fact exists. Therefore, there are only legal issues for the court to decide, and no trial with a jury (or other fact-finder) is necessary.

You need to keep all of the above in mind when you're crafting the "conclusion" sentences.

PART II:

To help you, I've prepared some sample conclusion sentences that work well in summary judgment briefs:

For P's MSJ (on P's claim):

- "The undisputed facts establish P's claim as a matter of law."
- "On this record, no reasonable jury could find in D's favor."

For D's opposition to P's MSJ:

- "P has failed to set forth sufficient evidence to prove her claim as a matter of law."
- "There are disputes on several material facts that a jury must resolve, making summary judgment inappropriate."

For D's MSJ (on P's claim):

- "P has failed to produce sufficient evidence on which a reasonable jury could find in her favor at trial."
- "No material fact disputes exist, such that D is entitled to judgment as a matter of law."

For P's opposition to D's MSJ:

- "There are too many material factual disputes for judgment to be entered as a matter of law."
- "P has adduced sufficient evidence on which a reasonable jury could find in her favor at trial."

9.2 How to find model briefs

When you find a case with facts and issues similar to those in your spring LRW assignment:

Pull the underlying briefs from the real-life lawyers from the cases.*

These lawyers were discussing the EXACT SAME issues you have to write about in your brief.

- Use their citations to help hone the rest of your research.
- Notice how they structure their legal analysis.
- Pick up on how they use words together.
- Learn their transition phrases.
- Copy their word cadence.
- Mimic their style.

Don't write your spring brief alone.
Do it the way lawyers have done all along.

You are training to become a lawyer, aren't you?
So, start training yourself!

***

PS—The briefs should be accessible online. On the main WL page, under "Content Types," one option is "Briefs," which has appellate briefs, and another option is "Trial Court Documents," which has lower-court briefs. Search by case name or cite, and you should be able to pull samples pretty easily. Assuming your professor's rules allow it, you might also try the 800 numbers for WL research support; the librarians at both WL and Lexis have historically been eager to explain how to find things.

PPS—Obviously, there is danger in relying on any model, so please use your judgment. Never rely on someone else's research alone; you must read and analyze every case cited and make your own evaluation as to the soundness of the authoring firm's research. Finally, consider the reputation and writing acumen of the authoring attorneys when judging the stock you put in the grammar and writing style in their briefs.

*As with all of my tips, please do not do anything that would violate any of your professors' rules or any school policy. Given the developments in AI around the time of this book's release, your school may prohibit you from implementing this tip in your first year.

9.3 You never really know a case until you try to write about it

Dear 1L,

Hi. I hope you're hanging in OK. I've had students tell me they had some of their darkest days of law school when trying to get the brief done, and I know you're in pretty deep.

Please know that the court cases you're dealing with are NOT "simple and easy."

In fact, there are no "simple and easy" cases when you're writing about a brand-new area of law.

You have to teach yourself that law before you can decide what you want to say about it, much less write something persuasive about it.

When I had to write a brief on a legal topic I'd never written about before, I had to spend some time understanding each court case INDIVIDUALLY first, before I could make sense of a group of them.

It helped me to write out a full, formal description of the case in a scratch document. I know doing that will seem cumbersome to you, but the process of articulating what a court did in your own words—on paper, in full sentences—has two big positives:

First, it can help you cut through the noise in the case and get you focused on what matters most.

For me, writing up some cases in a separate document often ended up being the only way I could get a real handle on things. I found I never really "knew" a case until I went to try to write about it.

Second, writing up the cases individually can give you place-holder paragraphs to insert into your Argument section so you're not starting with a blank page when you go to write.

True, you'll have to shorten and tweak your descriptions for purposes of the final brief. But it's always easier to cut and condense than it is to add.

* * *

I'm sending you brain cells and good cheer.
This is a really brutal time of year.

~Amanda

9.4 Always give a case's procedural posture and who won

Every year in BigLaw (except perhaps 2009), there was a fresh crop of first-year associates.

You could feel the buzz of beginnings in the air on Day 1. There was nervous energy and excitement, and they brought a powerful injection of enthusiasm into our department.

But there was a serious mistake they'd all always make.

It happened when they wrote up case-law research for me—whether in an email, a research memo, or a draft brief.

The mistake was this: they failed to specify any case's procedural posture or what the prevailing party "won."

It caused me so much frustration.
Please don't make this mistake.

You must make clear both the procedural posture and the outcome for every single case that you use as a comparator case to your case.

If you are writing on a summary judgment motion (MSJ), for example, you must specify whether the cases you discuss actually granted or denied the moving party's motion. Sometimes, you might get a helpful holding on one issue, but the case ends up going the other way on a second issue that becomes dispositive.

Those details are critical to include so that your reader knows how much weight to give the case.

Don't make a court clerk or law firm partner have to look up the cases you cite just to determine how they came out.

Remember, your reader is busy. Your reader has little time and little patience. Your reader will become annoyed with you if you make things hard.

Always make your reader's experience as simple and pleasurable as possible.

I am sending you fortitude and determination during your

brief-writing process. I know it can become all-consuming, and I'm rooting for you behind the scenes.

9.5 The problem with "the court found"

In your briefs this spring, don't use the verb "find" to describe a court's legal conclusions.

"But Amanda," you say, "many lawyers—even judges—use 'find' generically to describe the actions courts take."

- I know. You are right about that. But that does not make using "find" right.

An appellate court doesn't "find" anything. It renders conclusions of law, not fact.

Trial courts don't "find" facts most of the time, either. On a motion for summary judgment, for instance, trial courts make rulings based on law. No facts are "found."

To be sure, there are non-jury bench trials and other miscellaneous proceedings where trial courts make factual findings.

But unless you're dealing with one of those, writing "the court found" is just sloppy.

The court cases you're dealing with for your advocacy brief this semester involve decisions on legal principles, not findings of fact.

So use a verb other than "find" when discussing what the courts did.

Try a synonym, such as "rule," "conclude," "determine," "decide," "hold," "reason," or "explain."

9.6 Sample CREAC transition phrases

One problem with the CREAC method taught in law school is that students tend to write paragraphs that are deserted islands.

Each paragraph may be correct in terms of fulfilling the role of a letter in CREAC, but no paragraph has any relationship with the one before it or the one after it.

You're at a disadvantage because you're new to this; you don't have an arsenal of go-to phrases you can draw on for use in your brief when you need to pivot from one topic to the next.

Please borrow some of mine:

A. Transition from your legal rule/explanation section to your discussion of court decisions:

- Under these legal standards,
- Applying these rules,
- When considering these factors,
- Courts have applied these standards to conclude that...
- In application, these legal tests have led courts to...
- Consistent with these principles,
- According to these requirements,

B. Transition from discussion of one favorable case to another:

- Similarly,
- The court in [case 2] likewise ruled that
- The court reached a similar result in [case 2]
- Also instructive is [case 2]
- Second,
- Consistent with the reasoning of [case 1] is [case 2].

C. Transition from favorable cases to unfavorable ones:

- It is expected that [opponent] will raise
- Nevertheless,
- By contrast, where the facts are [not like yours],
- Conversely,
- To be sure,
- The cases that go the other way are...

D. Transition from explanation of cases to application to your facts:
- So too here,

- As in _______, the plaintiff/defendant here...
- In the same way,
- Much like _______ was true there, here...

E. Transition from application to conclusion:

- And so,
- Therefore,
- Thus,
- As a result,
- In the end,
- Overall,
- Accordingly,
- Boiled down,

Use these, or create your own. But do use something. Otherwise your brief will be very dry and sandy for the reader. :)

9.7 Table of Contents: the most important part?

It's a mistake to blow off your Table of Contents (TOC). Don't leave it until the last minute, either. The TOC may even be the most important part of your brief.

It's likely the very first thing a court will read, and that makes it prime real estate for starting to persuade.

- Don't lose the chance to make a convincing first impression.

If your TOC gives the court everything it needs and sells your side's position, the court should be leaning toward delivering your side victory before your introduction even starts.

To create a winning TOC:

- Do write persuasive point headings that read well together, one after another, and tell a cohesive, comprehensive story.
- Do make the page(s) as visually appealing as possible.
- Do NOT permit any typos or formatting errors.
- Do NOT wait until the final hours to start it. (It will take you much longer to prepare than you think, and it needs to sell your case.)

9.8 Statement of Facts: don't let it read like a rap sheet

The "Statement of Facts" in your brief should not read like a rap sheet. Instead, you need to tell a story that engages your reader and elicits sympathy for your client.

To achieve this goal, you need to make your writing "flow" between sentences. Try these five bridging techniques:

1. Repeat a word from the end of a sentence to start the next.

ORIG: John went to the store. He bought bread.
REVISED: John went to the store. At the store, he bought bread.

- This technique bridges the gap between the two sentences for your reader, providing a smoother passage from one sentence to the next.

2. Start sentence 2 with a catchall word or phrase that represents an idea from sentence 1.

ORIG: John went to the store to buy bread. John failed because the store was closed.

REVISED: John went to the store to buy bread. His mission failed because the store was closed.

- The word "mission" at the start of sentence 2 is a catch-all that represents the entire idea from sentence 1 and carries it forward, providing a bridge into sentence 2.

3. Start sentence 2 with a "this" or "that" in front of either:

a. a repeated word from sentence 1 (method 1), or
b. a catch-all that stands for an idea in sentence 1 (method 2).

E.g.,

A: John went to the store to buy bread. This bread would be a key part of the delicious brunch he was planning.

B: John went to the store to buy bread. That mission was unsuccessful because the store was closed.

- "This bread" and "that mission" both link the idea from sentence 1 into the idea of sentence 2.

4. Start sentence 2 with a standalone "this" or "that," where the context makes clear what "this" or "that" refers to.

E.g.,

John went to the store to buy bread. That was his only mission for the morning.

- Here, "that" can stand alone to represent the entirety of sentence 1, in that the "that" refers to the whole idea of going to the store to buy bread. By using "that," you carry the whole idea of sentence 1 into sentence 2.

5. Finally, it's also fine if you simply add an express linking or transitional word at the start of sentence 2 to show its relationship with sentence 1.

"However" and "But" are two such transition words.

ORIG: John went to the store to buy bread. He ended up buying milk in addition to bread.

REVISED: John went to the store to buy bread. But he ended up buying milk, too.

* * *

RECAP: Don't just recite facts. Tell your client's story. Make it flow.

9.9 Introductions: the hardest part to start

Some writers spin their wheels trying to create the perfect opening for the introduction to their brief. You know, that catchy one-liner that seemingly encapsulates the gist of the whole case at once, often using analogy, metaphor, or another literary device to imprint the writer's point.

I used to do that, too.

It's almost always a mistake. (Reply briefs excepted, sometimes.)

Here's why.

Unlike you, who feel so deeply steeped in the details of your case, your reader has no clue. Reading your introduction may even be your reader's very first introduction to the case.

Without knowing the parties or what the case is about, your reader can't possibly appreciate the import of a one-sentence zinger. It will fly over their head, confuse them, or even annoy them.

Just start simply. That is perfectly acceptable.

Craft a few sentences that say what the case is about, who the parties are, what happened, and what the issues are.

> *The value of these [introductory] words depends on clarity.*
> *If readers do not quickly understand the context and the issue, they*
> *will struggle even more as they plunge into the document.*

> —Hon. Robert E. Bacharach, *Legal Writing 1* (2020).

> *Judges crave an immediate sense of overview. At the beginning of*
> *a brief...[t]hey want to know what kind of case this is and what*
> *issues the brief addresses.*

> —Hon. Ruggero J. Aldisert, *Winning on Appeal: Better Briefs*
> *and Oral Argument* 182 (1992) (quoted in Brian A. Garner,
> The Winning Brief 132 (3d ed. 2014)).

True, there will be cases that call for a special flair of rhetoric in your opening line, and if you're an experienced legal writer and litigator, you might just pull it off. But far more often than not, the "clever" one-liner you've become enamored with will land on deaf ears. Worst case scenario, it will miss its mark.

So I wouldn't try it. The last thing you want to do is lose your reader in your opening sentence.

9.10 Introductions: what to include

Beyond your opener, what should go into your introduction?

First, you should be aware that some professors call the entire introduction a "thesis paragraph"; others refer to it as the "CR" part of the CRAC or CREAC structure; others call it a "rule statement"; and still others call it the "main umbrella paragraph."

I use "introduction" or "introductory paragraph" to refer to the very first substantive paragraph of a brief that precedes the statement of facts. I use "umbrella paragraph" to refer to the little paragraphs at the start of all sections in your argument that contain subsections.

These are the standard, recommended elements for an introduction:

1. A thesis statement that asserts how the main issue(s) should be decided, how those issues relate to each other (in the case of a brief with more than one main issue), and an assertion of how the court should rule.

2. A description of the legal rule or rules the court should use to decide the issue(s). In the introduction, you should just reference your main arguments and not the subsections of those arguments. In the umbrella paragraph before discussion of the first main issue, you will reference the applicable sub-issues to the first main issue, and so on.

3. A brief explanation if any parts of the rule will not be addressed in your brief.

4. A roadmap to the argument section of your brief that describes the organization of the argument section of the brief.

5. An introduction to your theme. This element is optional, but will make for a much stronger brief. Again, follow your professor's specific advice.

6. A discussion of any applicable policies. This element is optional, and whether to include will depend on your particular issues and any theme you've chosen for the brief.

Please note that your professor may insist that the above ingre-dients come in a specified order, but in general, any order is acceptable.

9.11 What goes in an umbrella paragraph?

The umbrella paragraph that goes after the word "Argument" and before your first heading will be similar to the introduction to the brief and contain the same ingredients. That said, an umbrella paragraph usually contains more pointed, fact-based reasoning because you will now have set forth the facts in full, and you may also present the content in a different order than you did in the introduction.

The mini umbrella paragraphs that go below your main headings and before two or more subheadings in a particular section of your brief should be limited to the issues in that particular section, but otherwise will contain the same general elements as the larger umbrella paragraph and introduction. You'll want to identify the particular issues you'll discuss in the section and how you think the court should come out on them. These paragraphs are typically only one to three sentences.

You will likely find yourself being repetitive in all these umbrella paragraphs, but that is OK. You want each section of your brief to be complete and able to stand on its own, because many readers will jump around and read sections at different times.

Ten ways to slay your oral argument

It's normal to be nervous for your first oral argument. It's a big unknown because you've never done it before. But that won't matter if you're the most prepared person in the argument room.

Here are 10 tips to help you prepare.

1. Know Your Case Cold.

Master the facts, the law, the record. You need to know them inside and out. Know where all the dead bodies are, too. Force yourself to practice answering the hardest questions you pray you won't be asked. (You likely will.)

2. Prepare for a Dialogue, Not a Speech.

The best oral arguments proceed like a conversation. Expect a back-and-forth, and prepare accordingly. Giving a memorized speech will not be persuasive, and you often won't be given the chance. IRL, you never know when you'll get a cold bench (i.e., one that asks few, if any, questions), so you should be prepared with a series of points you want to get across, even though you likely won't get the chance.

3. Keep it Simple.

Distill your argument into two to four primary points. Know them by heart. Make them a recurring refrain you can keep coming back to during the Q&A.

4. Be Ready to Go Out of Order.

With your primary points, don't be wed to a particular order. If you have points A, B, and C, get comfortable transitioning from B to A, or from C to B, etc.

If a judge asks something that seems out of logical order, be flexible. Never say, "I'll get back to that," or "I will answer that after telling you this." Just answer the question.

5. Make the Court's Job Easier.

Judges see oral argument as a way to help them write an opinion.

They want to get that opinion right, so you need to be prepared to articulate the legal test you'd apply and how future cases would fare under that test (especially on appeal, where decisions bind future litigants).

6. Be Ready for Hypos.

Judges see oral argument as a way to learn. They want to understand and probe the reach of your position as it applies to other fact patterns. Judges often do so through hypothetical questions. Prepare for these.

If a judge asks a hypothetical question, never answer, "That's not what happened in this case."

7. Never Dodge a Question.

If a judge asks a yes or no question, the first words you say should be yes or no. Only then should you elaborate, to try to advance the ball your way.

8. Become Familiar with the Argument Room.

Visit it in advance. Learn where you will sit and where you will stand. Become comfortable at the podium. Spend time in the room. Absorb it. Own it. This will help you feel more comfortable on argument day.

9. See How It's Done.

Seeing how other arguments have gone will help you in your own. Try videos of top students competing in moot court competitions to watch oral advocacy in a setting like yours. Or read transcripts of past arguments in cases like yours—see what worked, what didn't, and get ideas and inspiration.

10. Practice, Practice, Practice.

As with all skills, the best way to master oral argument is to practice. If you can arrange a parlay with friends, that works best. You will be sure to get asked questions you haven't yet considered. And if practice with others is infeasible, a mirror works, too. Stand and deliver your opening points.

CHAPTER 10

SPRING WRITING TIPS

10.1 "Because" is trouble after a negative verb

"Because" is one of the most important words in legal writing. But after a negative verb, "because" becomes bad news.

Bad-news examples:

1. She was not promoted because she is female.

- Was she promoted? That isn't clear.
- Perhaps she was promoted, just not because she is female.

Try these options instead:

Because she is female, she was not promoted.

-or-

She was promoted, but not because she is female.

2. John did not go to court because of the litigation.

- Did John go to court? Again, it's not clear.
- Perhaps he did go to court, but he went for a reason other than the litigation.

Try these options instead:

Because of the litigation, John did not go to court.
-or-
John went to court, but the litigation was not the reason.

Final point:

Most say that in addition to restructuring negative-because sentences as shown above, you can also remove ambiguity by adding a comma before the "because."

I disagree.

To be sure, it's fine grammatically to add a comma:

She was not promoted, because she is female.
-or-
John did not go to court, because of the litigation.

But the comma looks awkward to me. That alone could give your reader pause and make them question your sentence's meaning.

So I'd stick with rearranging over comma'ing.

10.2 Can a preposition end a sentence?

"You should never end a sentence with a preposition." Were you taught this rule, too? Well, it's crap.

Here's evidence, with some important caveats to think about and references for further reading.

*

Bryan A. Garner, *Garner's Modern Legal English Usage*, 4th ed. (2016), pp. 723:

The spurious rule about not ending sentences with prepositions is a remnant of Latin grammar, in which a preposition was the one word that a writer could not end a sentence with...

But if the SUPERSTITION is a 'rule' at all, it is a rule of rhetoric and not of grammar, the idea being to end sentences with strong words that drive a point home...

Good writers don't hesitate to end their sentences with prepositions if doing so results in phrasing that seems natural.

*

Wayne Schiess, *Fine Points for Legal Writing* (2019), pp. 32:

Some professors and lawyers enforce a rule against ending a sentence, or even a clause, with a preposition...There is no such rule.

[But] ending a sentence with a preposition can be considered too informal, so if you're writing for a professor or lawyer who follows the rule, you should follow the rule, too.

*

Mignon Fogarty, Grammar Girl Quick and Dirty Tips, "Ending a Sentence with a Preposition," Dec. 3, 2020 (website accessed Oct. 20, 2022) (citing sources):

Yes, you can end a sentence with a preposition... Nearly all grammarians denounce any strict rule against sentence-ending prepositions, and any such rule is "a myth."

[But] the myth is so prevalent, there are times when you should

avoid doing it even though I'm saying it isn't wrong. For example, when you're writing a cover letter to a potential employer, don't end a sentence with a preposition.

* * *

As for me, I am always trying to become a better, more informed writer. But old habits die hard.

And so, I've been trying diligently for a while now to unlearn what I'd long been taught. (Five years of Latin, having a long-term client who enforced the "rule," and other influences did not serve me well in this regard.)

I still find myself regularly rearranging sentences to avoid sentence-ending prepositions—without awkward wording. I find that often, sentences simply read better once refigured to avoid the dilemma.

But I also know that my view on what "reads better" may be haunted by so many years of Latin-grammar and client-focused indoctrination.

What's your take on this one?

10.3 Take care with "as" clauses

Today I write about why you must be cautious when you start a sentence with the word "As" and then follow it with a noun and comma.

For example, "As plaintiff,...," "As a lawyer,...," "As the judge,..."

I call this category of opening clauses "As-Noun-Comma" clauses, or just "As" clauses, for lack of any official term.

I estimate that the grammar of four out of five legal writers goes out the window when they start a sentence with "As." Here are just a few examples I've seen lately:

1. As a published author, people ask me a lot of questions about how to get started writing a book.

2. As a trial lawyer, law students see me as an expert in civil procedure.

3. As a junior lawyer, one of the best ways to leave a good impression on supervisors is by properly managing files.

To be sure, as a reader, you can get the gist of the author's meaning, but none of the sentences seem quite right. They suffer the same grammatical defect for the exact same reason. If you can't detect it, read on.

The authors of the above three examples all forgot the golden rule for As-Noun-Comma Clauses:

RULE: The only word that should follow an opening "As" clause is a synonym for the noun or noun phrase that (1) follows the word "As" and (2) comes before the comma.

EXAMPLE 1

✗ So if I wrote, "As a former litigator and current legal writing coach, law students ask me a lot of questions...," that would be incorrect.

"Law students" are not a synonym for "a former litigator and current legal writing coach." The incorrect construction is problematic because it leaves the initial "As" thought incomplete. It can also create a miscue for the reader, who may expect the sentence to follow the norm of renaming the noun from the "As" clause immediately after the clause.

✔ A correct construction would be, "As a former litigator and current legal writing coach, I receive a lot of questions from law students."

In this correct construction, I've appropriately renamed "former litigator and current legal writing coach" with the synonym "I," because in my case, "I" is the same person as "former litigator and current legal writing coach."

EXAMPLE 2

Here's another example:

✘ As a law student, it is hard to have a writing competition right after exams.

I don't know what "it" is, but it isn't a law student.

Possible correct constructions include:

✔ "As a law student, I find it hard to have a writing competi-tion..." (if you are writing)
-or-
✔ "As a law student, you must find it hard to have a writing competition..." (if I am writing to you).

10.4 "As such" does not mean "therefore"

While you're thinking of "as" clauses, let's take one out of circulation.

It's "as such." Most people think it means "therefore," and they use it in sentences like:

"It rained. As such, we can't go play." That is just so wrong.

If you don't see right away why those sentences are incorrect grammatically when paired together, I recommend that you make a decision now to never use "As such." Use "Therefore." It's safer.

I will try below to explain to you what "as such" means, but I confess I've abandoned caring. The phrase is like nails on a chalkboard to me because I always know a grammatical error is undoubtedly coming next. The phrase also reminds me of my 1L legal writing instructor who liked to use it, so there's that shadow. But at the end of the day, it just doesn't come up much, and you can always use "Therefore" instead.

And so, the big takeaway is this: Put "as such" on the Do-Not-Use list. OK? You've got plenty else to worry about this year.

I've managed just fine never using it, even though I know how to if I want, so for you, just don't use it during 1L. You can decide if you want to learn and practice it sometime later on in life (or not).

***

For the daring:

"As such" means "in that capacity," or "in that respect."

It can only refer to the actors (noun subjects) themselves that carry out verbs. There is debate on whether it can also apply to adjectives that describe those actors. But "as such" can never be used to refer to a situation existing or to there "being" something.

For example, you CAN say,

"She was promoted to manager. As such, she supervised other employees."

- The "such" replaces "manager"/ "she" and therefore works.

"The night had become a force. As such, it was beating us back inside."

That works because the "night" is operating as an actor that the author has personified to be forcing them to do something.

The example below is questionable, but again, let's just not go there.

??? John was tired. As such, he felt too tired to play.

RECAP for purposes of 1L year: Never use "as such."

Capische?

10.5 Nothin's comprised of nothin'

If you are prone to writing "is comprised of" or "is comprised by," take note.

They are both always wrong.

Here's why.

"To comprise" = "to contain," "to consist of," "to be composed of."

All these sentences are correct:

- The whole contains its parts.
- The whole consists of its parts.
- The whole is composed of its parts.

- The whole comprises its parts.

There is no such thing as "is comprised by."

***

Correct examples:

- The brief comprises four main arguments.
- The committee comprises three subcommittees.
- The prior sentence comprised five words.
- The statute comprises four sections.
- Plaintiffs' argument comprises two flawed theories.

There is no such thing as "is comprised by" or "is comprised of."

I have yet to discover a clever memory device, but the best way to learn how to use a word is to start using it correctly and regularly.

For a while, you'll likely have to double-check the meaning each time. But eventually, it will become second nature. (That is how I learned it!)

PS—I am not a patent lawyer, but my understanding is that in that context, a key difference exists between "to comprise" and "to consist of."

- "To comprise" is "open." It connotes non-comprehensive-ness, so if an invention comprises elements A and B, the invention may also include other elements.

- "To consist of," by contrast, is "closed" and is comprehensive, so if an invention consists of A and B, the invention may not also contain other elements.

10.6 The Terminator Rule

I once had a BigLaw partner brandish an imaginary assault rifle and simulate a scene from Arnold Schwarzenegger's *The Terminator* when imparting feedback on my writing:

"Who are you, the Terminator?" she asked.

The partner was very senior, and she happened to be wearing a bright dress and ballet flats at the time, so her act would have been quite amusing if I weren't so terrified.

The point of her stunt was to show disdain for my sentence,

"The company terminated the plaintiff."

Instead, she urged, I must write,

> "The company terminated the plaintiff's employment."

I was a first-year associate at the time, and I obeyed, but I was seeing lawyers and judges use the word "terminate" as a synonym for "fire" all the time, so I was a bit perplexed.

1. "The company fired the plaintiff." *That works.*
2. "The company terminated the plaintiff." *Does that?*

Is the second sentence wrong?

Back to the partner. She got quite animated when explaining to me why—yes, absolutely—the second sentence was dead wrong.

"To terminate" means "to bring to an end," she explained. And as attorneys for a company defending an unlawful employment termination case, we absolutely did not want to suggest anything of the sort.

Well, she was right, and she made her mark on me. I've never written "terminated the plaintiff" (or anyone) ever again, and I can't imagine that I ever will. But I still see others do it all the time.

Do you use "to terminate" in place of "to fire"? Maybe you should stop, at least when it comes to the formal legal writing you'll be doing.

10.7 Was that "affect" or "effect"?

For most of my life, I avoided "affect" as a verb. I would use "impact," or just change the sentence around to avoid the decision.

But the verb "to impact" doesn't really mean "to affect." ("To impact" means to hit with force, or to jolt.) And sometimes my sentence-rearranging was awkward.

So my so-called solution didn't really work.

Being me, I then read dozens of articles by grammar tipsters. They offered lots of definitions, explanations, examples, and memory devices.

But nothing seemed to stick. I still had to double-check—these days, on Google.

But I finally thought of something that seems to have stuck (at least for a few years now):

"I must affect (influence) you to effect (bring about) change in you."

- The "a" comes before "e" in the alphabet, so "affect" comes before "effect" in the sentence.

Hoping it will stick.

Thought I would share in case you have been a Googler like me.

PS—In the above, I discuss only the verb forms of affect and effect. Both words can also both be used as nouns, but I've never had trouble distinguishing between the noun "effect" (a result or outcome) from the noun "affect" (an expressed or observed emotional response or attribute). ("Affect" as a noun is very uncommon.)

CHAPTER 11

ELEVATE YOUR WRITING STYLE

11.1 Let's talk sentence length

You've probably never thought much about your sentence length before, but you'll have to start in law school.

The main advice you'll receive is to make your sentences shorter. That is good basic advice—especially if you're coming from college and are used to writing long, intricate sentences—but it doesn't tell you the most important consideration.

You'll also see some numbers thrown around by legal-writing experts, including that a sentence should be about 14 words, that you should aim for an average of 20 words, and you should aim for 26 words or less, to name a few. Again, all sage advice, but not targeted at the worst sentence-length culprit.

That culprit is sameness. Your goal for sentence length should be variety—indeed, some creativity.

And so, yes, keep your sentence length shorter than you're used to, and perhaps when your length AVERAGE is calculated at the end of the day, around 20 words might be a good metric, but do NOT make all your sentences 20 words, or your brief will be painfully boring to read.

Below is a blurb that illustrates what I mean from Gary Provost's *100 Ways to Improve Your Writing*.

> This sentence has five words. Here are five more words. Five-word sentences are fine. But several together become monotonous. Listen to what is happening. The writing is getting boring. The sound of it drones. It's like a stuck record. The ear demands some variety.

> Now listen. I vary the sentence length, and I create music. Music. The writing sings. It has a pleasant rhythm, a lilt, a harmony. I use short sentences. And I use sentences of medium length. And sometimes when I am certain the reader is rested, I will engage him with a sentence of considerable length, a sentence that burns with energy and builds with all the impetus of a crescendo, the roll of the drums, the crash of the cymbals—sounds that say, "Listen to this; it is important."

So write with a combination of short, medium, and long sentences. Create a sound that pleases the reader's ear. Don't just write words. Write music.

—Gary Provost, *100 Ways to Improve Your Writing* (2019), pp. 58-59.

11.2 "Thus" and "therefore" have a request

I got a note from "thus" and "therefore" overnight. It seems they have teamed up to send this message:

1. "We are overworked."
2. "We are tired of being first in sentences."
3. "We would like to sit next to someone other than a comma for once."

I told them I would see what I could do.

So here's this to you, my dear legal writer:

We're relying on "thus" and "therefore" too often, and we're unimaginative when we are.

- "Therefore, the plaintiff's arguments are unpersuasive."
- "Thus, the court should grant the motion."

Blah, blah, blah.

Our sentences are grammatically correct, but they're also over-the-top predictable.

Such sentences make our prose plodding and uninspired if we don't inject some variety.

    a. You often don't need "thus" or "therefore" at all—or any substitute for them. You can be more convincing by just cutting them altogether, at times.

    b. But when something is absolutely needed to bridge your content flow, you have other options beyond "Thus,..." and "Therefore,..." to start sentences.

One is to use "And so" or "So" (no comma needed afterward) as a substitute for "Thus" or "Therefore."

This option is suggested by BriefCatch and is a good one, provided you're comfortable with the more informal style.

- "And so the plaintiff's arguments prove unpersuasive."
- "So the court should grant the motion."*

    {*I'm not sure I'd use "so" for such boilerplate, wrap-up sentences, but the word can work well in the body of a brief.}

A second option is to move "thus" and "therefore" to the middle of your sentences (no surrounding commas needed).

Doing so is less predictable and will add some variation to your sentence structure, which will improve your overall writing style.

Here are example sets using each word:

ORIGINAL: "Thus, we decided to delay the deposition."

TRY INSTEAD: "We thus decided to delay the deposition."

✖ NOT: "We, thus, decided to delay the deposition."

***

ORIGINAL: "Therefore, his counsel ceded to our demands."

TRY INSTEAD: "His counsel therefore ceded to our demands."

✖ NOT: "His counsel, therefore, ceded to our demands."

11.3 "However" is a snoozy sentence-starter

When I review your writing, one of the first things I do is reword almost all sentences that start, "However,…"

"But starting sentences that way is grammatically correct," you might protest.

And you'd be right. Even so, I suggest you limit your use of this sentence-starter.

There are four rules you need to know.

1. THE GRAMMAR RULE

The first rule is basic, but it's been a minute since middle school, so here's a refresher.

There are only three ways you can use "however" to show contrast or indicate a shift in direction.

These are all correct:

- ✔ P is this. However, D is that.
- ✔ P is this; however, D is that.
- ✔ P is this. D, however, is that.

This one is incorrect:

- ✘ P is this, however, D is that.

2. THE USAGE RULE

The word "however" without a comma means "in whatever way" or "to whatever extent."

Examples:

"However he travels there, he'll be late."
"Do it however you like."

So unless you intend that other meaning, always use a comma after "however."

3. A GREAT STYLE RULE

Some seem to slap a "However,…" at the start of every sentence that contrasts in some way with the sentence before it.

Although perhaps that's OK grammar-wise, using "However,…" haphazardly like that is not good style-wise.

"However,…" is not some all-powerful sentence-starter that will magically make your writing flow. In fact, many top legal writers shun the practice altogether (see Rule 4).

At the very least, add variety by placing "however" (surrounded by commas) in the middle of your sentences.

E.g., "Bob aimed for high quality in his posts. Mary, however, strove for consistency. Mary's approach ultimately begot better results."

Or try these other good alternatives to "However,…":

But
Yet
Still,
Even so,
All the same,
At the same time,
By contrast,

4. THE NEARLY-NEVER-HOWEVER RULE

Most advanced legal writers—especially those who do a lot of high-level brief writing or teach on the subject—tend to harbor strong views on whether it's preferable to start a sentence with "However,..."

To begin, I've never heard anyone lament NOT seeing "However,..." to start a sentence in a brief. On the other hand, if you use "However,..." to start a sentence, you risk the disdain of many experienced legal writers who loathe it.

We react: Yuck! Yawn! Middle school! Frog got your throat?

> *'However,' is a 'ponderous' way to [start a sentence].*

— Bryan A. Garner, *Garner's Modern English Usage* (2016), at 472.

"Ponderous" means slow, clumsy, dull, and laborious.

Yikes! That should be the last way you'd ever want to write!

With three plodding syllables and a pause for a comma, "However,..." also lacks "oomph."

Instead, try "But..." or "Yet..." (no comma). "But..." and "Yet..." each save you four letters and a comma. In a legal brief, that might mean saving several lines of text. Every little bit helps when you're trying to squeeze into a page limit.

I know that using "And" and "But" to start a sentence is what your middle-school teacher taught you never to do. That is OK. You can break that phantom "rule." It was likely designed to teach you to write in complete sentences.

Aren't you past that?

> *I love 'But' at the beginning of a sentence, and I never put 'However' at the beginning—almost never.*

—Justice Antonin Scalia (in Garner, 13 *The Scribes Journal of Legal Writing* (2010), at 60.)

NB—If you prefer "however" to show contrast, consider putting it in the middle of the sentence.

* * *

FINALLY, if you do use "However" at a sentence's start, always follow these guidelines:

✔ Use a comma.

The word "however," standing alone, is ambiguous. It can mean "by contrast" (most common), but it can also mean "in whatever way" or "to whatever extent."

- E.g., "However fast your SUV goes, it won't beat our Porsche."

The by-contrast use must be followed by a comma.
The in-whatever-way use must not.

✔ Do so sparingly.

You need variety.

Rule of thumb: Don't use more than one "However,..." sentence-starter in any brief.

Try it. I promise your brief will be better for it.

* * *

As for me, I don't think I ever use "However,..." when I write.
But I don't edit them all out of your writing I review.
I edit almost all of them out.
You should, too.

PS—Many other words—such as "nevertheless" and "nonetheless"—are best avoided for similar reasons. With "however," they share many shortcomings. But they're far less common. College students don't come to law school using "nevertheless" and "nonetheless" in the willy-nilly way they use "however." That's why I put focus on "however" above the others here.

11.4 "Utilize" won't make you sound smart

It's around this time every year that I start getting cranky about the word "utilize." Every new legal writer seems to write "utilize" a lot, and I don't understand why. If you're someone who's in the habit, please stop. "Use" is better. Here's why:

1. Using "utilize" for "use" won't make you sound smart.

More likely, you'll come off as "trying to sound smart"—perhaps smarter than you really are. That's a bad look.

Unless you are positive that in your legal context, your reader prefers "utilize" to mean "use"—does anyone?—just write "use."

2. "Utilize" doesn't only mean "use."

- "Utilize" can mean "to use something in a new or unsanctioned way." Similar meanings include, "to convert to an unintended use," and "to give use to something otherwise useless."
- "Utilize" can also mean "to make use of," or "to make useful," which is close to "use," but not quite.

Perhaps there might be an occasion to use "utilize" instead of "use" when you mean "to make use of" as something different than "use"? Even so, that will be most uncommon.

- When in doubt, stick with "use."

My conclusion is this:

If you intend "utilize" to mean something other than "use," then it's OK to use "utilize" instead of "use." Otherwise, if you mean "use," just write "use."

3. "Utilize" is a needlessly long, multisyllabic word for "use."

You don't have room to spare in legal writing. Cutting your writing to your reader's page requirements will be hard enough. So you definitely don't want to add unnecessarily long or complex words when you don't have to. "Use" saves four characters and two syllables over "utilize."

For further reading, see Ross Guberman, "Judges Speaking Softly,

What They Long for When They Read," 44 Litigation 4 (Summer 2018); *see also id.* ("'I loathe the word 'utilize.'")

11.5 Only snoots say "prior to"

Avoid using "prior to" as a synonym for "before" in legal writing.

It's stiff.
It's stilted.
It's stuffy.

"Prior to" will not make you sound smarter than "before."

"Prior to" will not impress your reader more than "before."

And even if "prior to" did achieve those goals, "sounding" smart and "impressing" your reader should never be goals. Your goal should be clarity above all else—with simplicity and conciseness next. To attain these goals, you'll gain nothing from using "prior to."

- "Before" means the same thing as "prior to."
- Writing "before" instead of "prior to" does not change the meaning.
- Writing "prior to" is less concise, less simple, and less direct.

You want to be MORE concise, more simple, and more direct. So lose the "prior to." "Before" works just fine, 99 percent of the time.

PS—Using "prior" as an adjective is fine. It's "prior to" that's on my chopping block!

11.6 Don't be willy-nilly with "while"

Don't create ambiguity by using "while" to mean "although."

The problem lies in sentences like this one:

"While the stove is off, the toaster works."

What does the writer mean, A or B?

A: "Although (=whereas) the stove is off, the toaster works."
 -or-
B: "When (~only when) the stove is off, the toaster works."

Here's another example: "While she's running for VP, her work mounts."

Is that:

A: "Although she's running for VP (e.g., not president), her work mounts."
-or-
B: "At the same time she's running for VP, her work mounts."

***

As readers, unless we have more context, we simply cannot know whether A or B is intended in either of the above examples. We may be unsure even with context.

The uncertainty arises because "while" has so many potential meanings, even when used as a conjunction (as in the above examples).

"While" means:

1. during the time that; at the same time as.
   Ex.: "Nothing much changed while he was away."

2. as long as
   Ex.: "While there's life, there's hope."

3. whereas (indicating a contrast); when on the other hand
   Ex.: "One person wants out, while the other wants to fight on."
   "The exam is hard for a novice, while it's easy for experts."

4. in spite of the fact that; although

> Ex.: "While he's respected, he's not well liked."

> "While plaintiff argues A, the evidence all shows B."

5. similarly and at the same time

> Ex. "While John liked the film, Jim loved it."

Only the third and fourth meanings are synonyms for "although."

By contrast, the meaning of "although," as a conjunction, is straightforward:

> "Although" = "whereas" or "in spite of the fact that."

MY TAKE:

Although legal scholars and usage experts disagree on the extent of the problem stemming from the use of "while" for "although," the clearest rule to avoid using "while" to mean "although" is this: Limit "while" to its temporal meanings.

Finally, if you think that rule is too draconian and you really must use "while" to mean "although," make sure you're not creating a stove-off-toaster-on problem!

11.7 Don't use "since" to mean "because"

In legal writing, you should avoid using "since" as a synonym for "because."

Wait, what's that you say?
- "Since" has been a good synonym for "because" since time immemorial?
- And "since" is a full syllable shorter, it has two fewer letters, and it sounds so much better than "because," you love to use it!

I know.

You're right.

But still.

Avoid "since" to mean" because" in legal writing. Here's why:

A: "Since" is a softer, less direct way to say "because."

Most of the time when legal writers use "since," they intend to convey causation. But there's no reason to beat around the bush with whether something did cause something else. Causation can be everything in the law.

"Because" clearly conveys causation.
"Since" suggests causation, but is less exact.

Be assertive in your legal writing. If you mean "because," just say "because."

B: "Since" can create ambiguity.

Using "since" to mean "because" forces your reader to guess your intentions. True, "since" can mean "because." But "since" can also mean three other things that have nothing to do with why something happened, only when it did:

- "while,"
- "after," or
- "at the same time."

Here are three sentences that use "since" in a way that's ambiguous:

1. "Since we discussed, I've changed my mind."
   - Do you mean you changed your mind after we discussed, or because we discussed?

2. "Since they ate breakfast, they were ready to leave."

   - Do you mean they've been ready to leave since the time that they ate breakfast, or that it was because they ate breakfast that they were ready to leave? A reader can't be sure. Sometimes, the writer might mean both.

3. "I listen to Taylor Swift more since someone got us tickets." (This one's true!)

   - Here, I mean "since" to mean both "after" and "because." It's OK that I'm imprecise. But in legal writing, every word should be precise and ambiguity-free.

Remember, your reader has a short attention span. Your reader will not appreciate being forced to spend additional time on your brief trying to figure out what you mean by "since."

Don't piss off your reader.
Obviously.
If you mean "because," write "because."

PS—Students also tend to use "as" and "for" to mean "because." Those two words are even more ambiguous than "since." Stick with "because" for clear, forceful prose.

THE EM-DASH HOW-TO

Before you use your next em-dash, make sure you know what you're doing.

I haven't seen an em-dash used properly in any of the student writing samples I've reviewed these past three years. Magazines and other periodicals follow different guidelines, so don't assume you know how to use them in legal writing.

So, what's an em-dash?

An em-dash—which looks like these here—is a punctuation mark that shows a break in a sentence.

All agree that you can use it in place of a comma or a colon, or as a pair in place of a pair of commas or parentheses.

The em-dash gets its name from the width it shares with the capital M.

Some people spell em-dash with a hyphen: "em-dash." I don't consider one spelling as more correct than the other.

Why use it?

An em-dash adds emphasis, draws attention to its content, and adds pizzazz to otherwise lifeless prose.

An em-dash can also improve readability, especially in an otherwise comma-clogged sentence.

Three common ways to use an em-dash:

1. Use an em-dash to set off words at the start or end of a sentence:

"*Palsgraff*—who could ever forget that case?"
"Who could ever forget the most famous tort case—*Palsgraff*?"

2. Use an em-dash in the middle or end of a sentence to define, conclude, emphasize, or explain the content that precedes it.

"The court awarded summary judgment—obviating the need for a trial."

3. Use a pair of em-dashes to set off mid-sentence content that is parenthetical, but that you want to amplify more than a pair of commas would, and not overshadow, the way parentheses would.

"The court relied on an outdated grammar book—the 1996 edition of *Woe is I*, by Patricia O'Connor—when interpreting the statutory text."

{There are also some other, uncommon and more technical em-dash uses. See Garner, Guberman, and Google for further reading.}

Two caveats:

1. Don't use more than one em-dash, or one pair of em-dashes per sentence; more than that is too much for the reader to keep track of.

2. Don't go crazy with em-dashes. Use them like a spice: a dash here and there is delicious, but don't drench. As with any device that adds emphasis, overuse defeats the purpose.

* * *

Will you try to use an em-dash the next time you write?

PS—Almost forgot: In legal writing, we generally don't use spaces on either side of an em-dash. Do it like this—OK? {The convention may be different for other types of writing.}

CHAPTER 12

EDITING SHORTCUTS

Dear 1L,

The first draft of your brief will be too long. (If it's not, there may be a bigger problem.)

The second draft of your brief will be too long, too.

This is just the way it is with legal writing. We have to fit SO much into just a few short pages. Your professor's rules are just like court rules that restrict the length of attorneys' briefs, so getting into the habit of cutting fluff will help you down the road, too.

The posts collected in this chapter are all designed to help you make cuts that will not detract from substance. I hope they will help you. Again, please budget your time.

~Amanda

12.1 Beware of wordy ways to say "because"

Before you turn in your draft, check to see if you've used any of these WORDY ways to say "because":

- In light of the fact that
- Due to the fact that
- On account of the fact that
- As a result of
- For the reason that
- On the grounds that

All these ways take a roundabout route to get to your point.

They're also clunky to read, and they add to your word count.

To be sure, there's a time and place for some wordy ways.

But it's not often.

And in legal writing, "because" is (almost) always better.

Might you swap out some wordy clauses from your writing today?

12.2 Minimize your expletives

If I told you to minimize your use of "expletives" in legal writing to help you cut words, you might retort, "I would never use expletives in legal writing."

Alas, but you do.
Here's what I mean.

Definition:

In addition to meaning a profane or obscene term, an "expletive" means any word or phrase in a sentence that supplies no independent, substantive meaning.

"There is," "There are," and "It is" are examples of expletives that appear regularly in writing.

They typically add nothing but fluff.

They drag down your prose and make it wordier.

Try dropping expletives from your sentences, and recast them with the subjects of the verbs doing the acting.

Examples:

"There is a delivery truck approaching our house now."
-becomes-
"A delivery truck is approaching our house now."

"There were three hotel employees who witnessed the event."
-becomes-
"Three hotel employees witnessed the event."

"It is agreed by all parties that the case should settle."
-becomes-
"All parties agree that the case should settle."

Exception:

As with all things involving subtlety, tone, cadence, nuance, etc., your sentences may sometimes call for expletives. But most of the time, expletives should be cut.

Cutting them is a great way to sharpen your prose and reduce your word count.

12.3 Shorten "in order to"

If you're someone who routinely writes the phrase "in order to," I suggest you reconsider.

Almost always, a simple "to" will do.

Try it when you edit your brief. Run a search for the phrase "in order to."

Substitute the simple "to."

You should find that your sentences still say precisely what they said before. But with more punch.

Example:

Jan went to law school in order to earn a JD. In order to get good grades, she made sure she slept eight hours each night, and she focused her study time between seven and ten each morning. She also exercised regularly in order to keep her anxiety in check.

Any "in order to" phrase that you'd keep in the above?

* * *

To be sure, on rare occasions, "in order to" can promote clarity—such as when a sentence already contains several "to" words, and you want to emphasize a change in focus or emphasis. But err on the side of banning "in order to."

Almost always, you'll maintain clarity. At the same time, you'll eliminate a stumble for your reader and shave two words.

12.4 Cut "the fact that"

"The fact that" is a clunky clause that says nothing. It's even worse when coupled with "despite," as in "despite the fact that…"

Here are some better options.

1. Drop "the fact." Just write "that."

Clunky: The fact that the professor said it was not what upset her. It was his tone.

Better: That the professor said it was not what upset her. It was his tone.

*

Clunky: He was dismayed by the fact that the court rejected his case.

Better: He was dismayed by the court's rejection of his case.

Better: The court's rejection of his case dismayed him.

2. Drop "despite the fact." Try "even though," or "although."

Clunky: Despite the fact that she had done nothing wrong, the police arrested her with all the others.

Better: Although she had done nothing wrong, the police arrested her with all the others.

Better: The police arrested her with all the others, even though she had done nothing wrong.

*

Clunky: The Supreme Court took this stance despite the fact that most Americans disagreed.

Better: The Supreme Court took this stance even though most Americans disagreed.

PS—There will be some occasions when you simply need to use "the fact that" for clarity. But always pause and ask yourself. Often a "that" will do just fine.

12.5 Try the "need not" sentence shortener

Next time you're trying to cut words or add some punch, try this:

Replace "is not required to" with "need not."

For example:

Instead of: "The defendant is not required to disprove the plaintiff's claims."

Try: "The defendant need not disprove the plaintiff's claims."

This edit is now a current favorite of mine, as I only recently discovered it.

12.6 Five hacks to cut words

Here are five ways to shorten your memos to fit your page limit (without cutting substance).

1. Convert sentences to active voice.

"The boy hit the ball."

—is shorter than—

"The ball was hit by the boy."

2. Convert noun clauses to single verbs.

make arrangement for → arrange

provide a description of → describe

3. Convert "of the" clauses into shorter possessives.

the qualities of a person → the person's qualities

the reasoning of the court → the court's reasoning

4. Remove adverbs.

worst offenders = very, clearly, plainly

5. Avoid starting sentences with "It is," or "There are."

"There are three factors that courts consider. They are:..."

—is longer than—

"Three factors the court considers are..."

BONUS: The above will also make your writing better!

12.7 More sultry sentence slicers

A sultry summer Sunday makes a tough day for legal writing.

But it's no picnic for a day of legal reading, either.

So strip some weight from everyone's load. Try these five sentence shorteners:

TOO HEAVY	→	LIGHTER
1. Despite the fact that	→	Even though
2. In the event that	→	If, Should

3. Is able to   →   Can

4. For the purpose of   →   For, To

5. An adequate number of   →   Enough

What heavy-handed phrase would you add to the "too heavy" list?

Happy sentence-stripping!

12.8 Try my editing P-E-N

We've all been there: The brief is done, but it's several pages too long. You've got a few hours to try to cut it before the filing deadline, and you can't afford to lose substance.

What's your first move?

Try my P-E-N approach. It kills the culprits behind three biggies that add unnecessary words:

- Passives
- Expletives
- Nominalizations

1. PASSIVES. (Culprit: "by the")

Root out passive voice by searching for sentences containing "by the." That's the most common signal for passive voice. Passive voice is always LONGER than active voice.

"The bill was passed by the Senate." (Passive/longer)
"The Senate passed the bill." (Active/shorter)

2. EXPLETIVES. (Culprits: "It is" and "There are")

Both two-word phrases are almost always useless expletives. They take up space without adding value. Cut them, and make your subject carry out the verb.

✘ "There are three factors that courts consider. They are:..."
✔ "Three factors the court considers are..."
✔ "The court considers these three factors:..."

3. NOMINALIZATIONS. (That's just a fancy way to say clunky noun clauses that can be converted into verbs.)

make arrangement for → arrange
provide a description of → describe
take the deposition of → depose

Without the nominalizations, the texts are shorter.

Tackling the law-review competition

It seems cruel. Your "reward" for finishing the hardest year in law school is staying around to do a long Bluebook test and a big legal-writing project. I would be SO tempted to skip the whole thing.

BUT being on law review was, without doubt, the greatest highlight of my law-school experience—both short and longterm. I want you to have a chance at that.

So yes, I do think that doing the write-on competition is 100 percent worth it, as miserable as it may seem.

Here is some info that should help you at the start.

1.

You will receive a big packet of competition materials, and it will come to you electronically.

You will run out of printer toner making a hard copy.

Buy a backup cartridge now—and more paper, too.

2.

The materials will look voluminous, and the subject matter will not be an area of law you know anything about. Don't freak out or call it quits.

The packet is really no bigger than what you got for your 1L memo or brief; it's just that you're accustomed to gathering the material piecemeal.

The material isn't harder, either. You've had to figure out difficult legal issues and write about them a lot this past year. (You're a pro!)

You can do this one, too.

3.

Finally, if you have a separate Bluebook test, consider starting it first.

It's annoying and laborious, but it's not a heavy lift, brainpower-wise.

It may be easier to start there, while your mind comes down off Con Law and other difficult doctrinal topics.

I would start the Bluebook test and then save the rest to use for "brain breaks" later, when you are deep into legal analysis and need to step back and do something rote to let the analysis percolate.

***

I am so very proud of you for making it through this academic year. It's been an epic one, and you deserve a long, pampered vacation. But I'm with you in this until the end, and we've got one more piece to go.

PART IV: GETTING A JOB

CHAPTER 13

RESUMES

Dear 1L,

At first, you may not see the relationship between legal writing
and job applications, but I assure you the relationship is close.

The key traits of strong legal writing—clarity, brevity, and simplicity—all apply with equal force to each of the items in a typical 1L job-application packet (a resume, a cover letter, a cover
memo, and a legal writing sample).

Remember, too, that lawyers will likely not be the first readers of
your application.

It often will be reviewed first by a non-attorney, such as a recruiting manager, a professional development director, or someone
from the firm's HR department.

These early readers act as gatekeepers who screen and "shortlist"
candidates for the attorneys on the hiring committee. You thus

need to craft your application with both a legal and non-legal audience in mind.

The following letters, checklists, and tips are designed to help you do that.

~Amanda

13.1 Why your resume needs to be perfect

I could talk till I'm blue in the face about why your resume actually needs to be perfect in form, but I thought it would be more effective to share with you a letter I wrote to 3Ls in the early fall of 2023.

Please don't let yourself be someone to whom such a letter would apply. Get your resume right the FIRST time around.

Dear 3L,

If you struck out at OCI,
If you're not getting interviews, or
If you're not proceeding past the first round,
The answer may be as simple as your damn resume.

And I don't mean your GPA, experience, or law school cache.

I mean your resume.

In the past few months, I've seen several jobless 3Ls' resumes that have broken my heart. This is after these resumes have been through multiple career-services-office reviews, after these resumes have been sent to hundreds of law firms and other prospective employers, and long after the students have been through the formalized OCI process.

And yet,
I'm still finding typos.
I'm still finding formatting errors.
I'm still finding awkwardly constructed bullet entries.
And more.

PLEASE examine your resume again.
Read it aloud.
Read it backward.
Put it in a different font.
Blow it up to 200 percent and scrutinize.
Let as many friends and family members as possible review it.

Just PLEASE make sure it's not as simple as the damn resume itself. You've worked too hard for that.

~Amanda

13.2 How to align your employment dates

If I were to review your resume right now, I can guess what I'd find.

You know all those employment-date ranges you have going down a column on the far right side?

You've been tabbing over and adding spaces before to try to make the dates all end in a line, flush right, right?

> (When I turn on Word's "Reveal Formatting" feature, I see all the little arrows and dots. I sigh and wish you'd been taught this rule, but alas…)

RULE: Tabbing and spacing over will NEVER make your dates align right.

Instead, you'll have a wavy row of dates that look messy and unprofessional.

Here's the BETTER WAY:

1: Put your cursor right before the text you want at the end at the right margin.

2: Go to > FORMAT > TAB, and then select CLEAR ALL TABS.

3: Staying on the same screen, go to > SET TAB. Select it and type in 6.5 (for standard margins); check ALIGNMENT: RIGHT & NO LEADER.

4: With your cursor still placed right before the text you want to move to the right margin, hit the TAB button.

And voila!

13.3 Aim for brevity in your experience entries

As you start to update your resume, your content will get denser, and your text will get longer.

How can you fit everything in?

Save space by cutting out these often unnecessary words:

- the
- a
- an
- of

the, a, an

In a resume entry—much like in the parentheticals you write to describe court cases—you rarely need to use these sorts of introductory words before nouns. (These words are technically called "articles.")

of

The word "of" is another culprit behind resume clutter. Change your word order to create a possessive form that is tighter and just as clear.

COMBINED EXAMPLES*

{*I'm not saying these examples are perfect. I'm merely trying to illustrate.}

1.

ORIGINAL:

"Supervised the team of paralegals to conduct a research project in regards to a motion for summary judgment for the manager's presentation to the board of the agency."

REVISED:

"Supervised paralegal team to research summary judgment

standards for manager's presentation to agency board."

-or-

"Led paralegals' summary judgment research for manager report to agency board."

No meaning is changed. No clarity is lost. But the revised versions are shorter and crisper.

2.

ORIGINAL:

"Attended meetings of the committees and agencies to prepare a report on the next steps for completion of the project."

REVISED:

"Attended committee and agency meetings to prepare report on next steps for project completion."

Again, the revised versions are shorter and punchier.

*

Might you try to make your resume more concise and engaging today?

13.4 Generalities will get you nowhere

In your experience entries, try to be specific about what tasks you actually completed, as opposed to writing what tasks you were "responsible for."

Think about your future interviewer, and give them a good script to ask you about.

You also want to stand out from the crowd, and the only way to do that is by narrowing your experience entries to fit you, specifically.

For example:

DON'T just say you researched "legal issues." Tell them WHAT specifically you researched and what it was for.

E.g.,

"Researched standards for class certification to include in employer's motion to dismiss race-discrimination claims."

"Researched case law interpreting state anti-racketeering statutes and composed memorandum of law for use in case status conference."

Your interviewer will find the specifics much more interesting, and they'll distinguish you from everyone else.

13.5 Form can matter more than substance

These final two tips may cause you to think I'm being a nit-picker, but what your resume looks like can make the difference in whether you get that interview.

When you're reviewing a big stack of resumes—the way the intake person will for prospective employers—you tend to pick up on little formatting details. You don't want to give that reviewer any reason not to endorse you.

One check you may not think to do targets the formatting of your punctuation marks.

If you have commas, semicolons, or periods at the end of bolded, underlined titles, is the punctuation also bolded and underlined?

Should it be?

- I prefer that it not be, but whatever you do, be consistent throughout.

If you place a period at the end of one bullet in an entry, make sure you end all other bullets that way.

If you want to use curly quotes instead of straight quotes—which I recommend—make sure they're consistent. I regularly see resume writers switch back and forth.

(There are countless other examples of little punctuation things like these. Try to proofread your resume backwards, aloud, or presented in a different-color font if you're having trouble picking up on little mistakes.)

Finally, hold your resume up to light and ask these questions:

- Does it require a magnifying glass to decipher?
- Does it look like a big wall of text?
- Is it taxing to keep track of what line you're on?
- Is there any white space, where weary readers' eyes can rest?

You likely won't understand this yet, but most of us get far-sighted past 42. Even with glasses on, reviewing a densely packed, resume in 10 pt. font can be daunting and frustrating.

The last thing you want your reviewer to feel is daunted or frustrated! So please use a bigger font and cut more useless words!!

Cover letters: be different!

$\mathbf{D}$ear 1L,

I don't give out model cover letters for a reason.

A "model" is the antithesis of what any cover letter should be.

Instead, your cover letter should scream:

"I'm different; I'm better; you want me; you want only me!"

To be sure, you need to format traditionally and use formal prose, but in terms of what you say after that, you need to stand out from the pack.

You need to be unique.

You need to go beyond the boilerplate.

You need to write a cover letter that no one else could write.

Here are five tips to help do it:

*

1. Be confident.

Approach each cover letter as if you are a highly credentialed, sought-after candidate.

- Do not let mediocre grades douse your ability to craft engaging copy, and do not downplay. Focus on your strengths and demonstrate the value you can bring.

*

2. Be enthusiastic.

I don't care if your grades are As or Cs, and I don't care if you are applying to one firm or 100. You should approach each as if it's your #1 choice.

- No, don't say the firm is your #1 choice if it's not true, but ask yourself whether you're really sure. A firm that you might gloss over in the first instance can end up being your number one bet in the end. There's simply no reason to give away that you plan to turn an offer down before you know the full extent of your options.

It's often the firm that ends up choosing you, not the other way around.

*

3. Be specific about the firm.

Research and find out something specific about the firm that makes it your top choice (as opposed to every other firm).

- Force yourself to find a distinguishing firm trait.

If your letter could easily be sent to several other firms, you haven't found something specific enough.

*

4. Be specific about yourself.

Strive to find something about you that would be hard for someone else to replicate.

For example, don't just write that you've gained analytical and legal-writing skills from your law school classes or that you know how to research on WestLaw. Everyone else can say that, too.

To help generate ideas for unique content, you might try asking yourself these questions:

What is something you've done in the last year (or two years, or five, ten, etc.) that your classmates have not done?

What is something specific you plan to do with your law degree that no one else can say?

What is some trait you've developed based on past events that no one else can talk about in the same way?

*

5. Inject some personality.

What's something interesting or funny that has happened to you? Any story will do.

- Tell it briefly, and then tie it to some specific trait about you, your background, or your achievements that makes you a top candidate for that firm.
- Anecdotes let your personality come through and distinguish you from others.

Personal stories are gold.

***

RECAP:

You're adding your resume to a big stack.

You need to stand out from the pack.

Be YOU, and you'll see.
You might even, if you dare,
add a dash of creativity!

~Amanda

CHAPTER 14

WRITING SAMPLES

14.1 How to create a writing sample

If you use your 1L memo or brief as a writing sample for job applications, you have some work to do before sending it to employers. Here are the six key steps:

1. Incorporate all prior feedback.

The first step is incorporating the final corrections and edits from your teaching assistant (TA) and professor.

2. Choose which sections to cut.

If your sample is longer than the required page length, decide which section to cut and how to edit for overall flow, so that cutting section(s) doesn't make things too hard for your reader to follow.

Here are four ways I've seen recent writing-sample excerpts miss the mark:

- They don't make clear who you represent or what you seek.
- The facts section is omitted, leaving no framework for the case.
- The defined terms are cut when a section is omitted.
- The legal standard is omitted, but there's no succinct synopsis of it before the argument, so the points don't make sense.

3. Add page numbers.

Nothing frosts a reader more than having to read something with no page numbers. They are absolutely essential.

Start page 1 on the first page of your brief's text.

- The cover memo, title page, and tables of contents/authorities are NOT included in the pages that count toward the page limit.

4. Put your name on the writing sample itself.

Many of the writing samples sent to me included exam numbers only, with no way to know which one corresponded to which student. I had to go through several emails after printing the samples to figure out who had sent them. A law-firm attorney might not bother.

Don't let your writing sample fall through the cracks among the hundreds, even thousands, that a firm may receive.

- Include your name clearly on the first page of your brief. (It's not enough to include it only in a cover memo.)
- Better yet, create a small footer with your first initial and last name. That way, if any pages get separated, they are easily put together again.

5. Change citations and other underlining to italics.

I know you're required to underline for legal writing class, but for the writing sample you'll send out with your resume, you should use italics.

In the real world, no one underlines. We all use italics.

Benefits:

- It's faster to type.
- It avoids the look of text that's cut up with choppy underlines.
- You don't need to know if you underline the period after Id.
- It looks more professional.
- It forces you to check your citations closely. You'll find mistakes.

6. Read your sample again closely to fix all the typos and awkward sentences. I promise you that many will still exist. While you're at it trying to spot errors, you might as well read each sentence again. I bet you can find how to cut more words.

14.2 Include a short cover memo

It's best to include a short cover memo with the writing sample you send to prospective employers.

Why should you include one?

Two reasons:

1. A cover memo is a golden opportunity to set the stage and to start "making friends" with your reader.
2. It's a lot easier to do a superior writing job within a short cover memo than the first paragraph of a formal memo or brief—especially when you're new to legal writing. You want your captivating style to be the first thing your reader/prospective employer sees of your writing.

Overall, you want to aim to answer two questions in this cover memo.

What does my reader need to know before starting my brief?

-and-

How can I interest my reader to be enthusiastic about my brief?

Your cover memo should remove all potential confusion and frustration that your reader could feel when starting on page 1 of the brief itself. (Same goes for memos, law review articles, and other forms of legal writing samples.)

Here's the specific type of substantive content to include:

1. An explanation of when and for what purpose you wrote the sample.
2. A short description of the topic about which you wrote, the parties and issue involved, and which side you represented, if any of that information would be necessary or helpful for the reader's orientation.
3. A statement that you have received permission to use the sample (if required).
4. An assertion that the sample is substantially your own work (if required).
5. An indication that the sample is a shorter excerpt from a longer piece (if applicable).

***

Beyond that, try to be a little original in what you say—including in your sentence structure, word choices, and style. In other words, try to make yours NOT read exactly like the model your school provided.

Cover memos can become bland and boilerplate if you don't give them due thought and care. Experiment with varying your sentence structure, word choices, and style to capture and build your reader's attention. Make your cover memo better written and clearer and more informative than everyone else's.

Finally, your OCI application packet should include parts that all look like they belong together: The "title," or "header," at the top center of your cover memo should look exactly the same as that on your resume and cover letter (name, phone, email, etc.).

* * *

Recap: Your goal is to get the reader to read and enjoy your writing sample. Don't miss out on the chance to achieve that goal in a cover memo.

PS—The cover memo does not count as a "page" and should not have a page-number footer.

Is Times New Roman (TNR) dead?

Dear 1L,

Today's message is inspired by a post I saw on LinkedIn and a new book called *Elegant Legal Writing* by Ryan McCarl.

The post said, "Friends don't let friends use TNR."

A 2L I know saw the post and promptly sent it to me by DM, asking, "Do you agree?"

I chuckled and said, "Yes, it's on the 'bad' list for briefs."

I then went to the comments under the original post and learned:

- He likes Book Antiqua
- Verdana is easier for dyslexics
- California rules say you should use TNR, Courier, or Arial
- Rhode Island rules require TNR—in 14 pt. font!

Feeling a bit confused, I consulted the advance copy of Ryan's book to see if it might address the topic, and BAM:

It gave me exactly what I needed—and I think it will be useful to you, too! It's got a handy list of fonts, "good" and "bad," and recommends these three:

- Century Schoolbook
- Palatino Linotype
- Bookman Antiqua

I followed up with that law student to confirm what I'd told him, and that's now one more law student looking forward to this book!

***

I don't think this new font information should affect anything you do for legal-writing class (I'm sure your prof has specific rules), but might you think to use one of the best fonts for the writing samples you send out?

(It can't hurt; I'm just saying.)

~Amanda

PS—Oh, and here are the fonts Ryan says you should NOT use:

- Arial
- TNR
- Courier New
- Calibri
- Verdana

CHAPTER 15

INTERVIEWS

15.1 Preparation

Until now, you likely haven't undergone many, if any, formal job interviews with BigLaw lawyers. Here's what to expect and five suggestions on how to prepare.

IN ADVANCE

1. Decide on three to four main points that you want to raise about yourself in the interview, regardless of the specific questions asked. Practice delivering answers on your main points.

- In this way, preparing for potential questions at a job interview is a bit like preparing for an oral argument in court. You want to make sure you hit your key points no matter what.

2. Research commonly asked interview questions, and draft answers to a dozen or so of them. That will get you doing something and calm nerves.

- Don't think of it as a waste of time, either. Even if your interviewer doesn't ask the specific questions you practice, getting the reps in will get you more comfortable answering any type of question.

BEFORE FIRST-ROUND INTERVIEWS

Screening interviews set in law-school interview rooms or virtually tend to be 20–30 minutes.

3. For every firm where you secure a first-round interview, conduct thorough research on both the firm and each specifically named interviewer.

- The goal is to have content that lets you lead the interview on your terms.

4. Prepare a one-page "cheat sheet" for each firm in which you have strong interest.

- The first round can feel a bit like 20- or 30-minute speed dating. You will not always have time to refresh regarding each firm right before your interview.

5. Make sure you have questions written out and fresh in your mind beforehand, because the second part of the interview will often be the interviewer asking what questions you have.

15.2 Interview tips

If you're feeling anxious about upcoming interviews for your first "legal" job, that's normal. Here's some advice from the 100 or so law-student interviews I've conducted.

1. BE YOURSELF.

The best job interviews proceed like a normal conversation. Do not recite rehearsed answers. Have a natural dialogue. Relax and talk to your interviewer just like you would a colleague of your parents or some random relative who's a lawyer.

- Should you prepare a canned answer? Yes, but prepare three or four. You don't want to sound stale. Have a few variations ready so you stay fresh.

- Smile. Not sure why it works, but injecting an energetic smile into the conversation periodically does wonders.

2. BE PREPARED.

The best students come thoroughly prepared. By this I mean that not only are they ready with topics to discuss, but they also have several intelligent questions ready to ask about my firm and me.

Read as much as you can about the employer. Do not ask, for example, whether the firm supports pro bono work, when an entire page on the firm's website provides detailed examples that you already should know about.

Learn about your interviewer. They are just human. Maybe their LinkedIn "About" section mentions they spent a year in another city or country where you have lived or visited. Maybe their profile mentions they love dogs, tennis, or jazz. All of those topics can produce excellent conversations.

3. ASK GOOD QUESTIONS.

Ask about your interviewer's career and how they came to work where they do. Also ripe fodder are cases handled, articles written, presentations delivered, etc.

People like to talk about themselves. Play to your interviewer's ego. If you can get them talking about interesting topics, they'll likely come away from the interview thinking that YOU are interesting.

4. SHOW MORE THAN TELL.

The best students support the adjectives they use to describe themselves with concrete specifics.

Better than saying you "have strong leadership qualities" is describing how you founded and headed a new student organization on campus, or how you rallied classmates behind a cause.

Better than asserting that you are a "good team player" is describing your role working on a recent group project.

Make sure you come in with several examples to illustrate your qualities, not just bare assertions that you have those qualities.

15.3 Don't do my downplay dance

I tend to do something bad that once caused me to bomb a job interview. It's a weakness of mine, and I didn't keep it in check. If you have this same tendency, don't let it ruin your interviews.

From a young age, I had learned I should downplay my accomplishments. To be humble. To be liked. The lesson was "taught" to me by those in the early-teen "cool" cliques. They all hated school. They hated their mothers. They hated almost any adult-sponsored thing.

I was an A student. I was one of those annoying kids who actually liked school. And I loved my mom. I wasn't "cool." Oh, but how I wanted to be. So I downplayed my successes to try to fit in.

Many of us have some similar version of the story, I would suspect. It is certainly not novel or unique. And many of us have adopted some version of downplaying to become more likable in various social situations. No one likes a braggart. But where is the line?

I don't know the answer. I still struggle to tout my accomplishments. I push down instincts to celebrate wins. I try to be humble, sympathetic, empathetic. To make others feel comfortable.

But one thing I know for sure:

Downplaying has no place in a job interview!

How did I screw up? It wasn't with the partners. Looking accomplished in front of them was easy—they were far more accomplished than me, so I didn't need to downplay myself to make them feel comfortable.

It was the "casual" associate lunch. I relaxed from my regular interview mode when seated at a restaurant with three female peers.

They seemed like close friends. I was uncomfortable. I didn't know how to act. So what did I do? I downplayed.

I wanted to fit in. I wanted to be liked. I met their questions about my experiences at a top NYC firm with mealy-mouthed answers:

- "They don't give associates that much responsibility in NYC firms compared with Philly firms."
- "I'm sure I did nothing nearly as exciting or skilled as you must do at your firm."

Oh, I went on and on.

I shudder when I think back. And, no surprise, a rejection letter arrived soon after: I didn't have the "experience" they were after.

I share my story for three reasons.

One, I hope it will remind you (if you are at all a downplayer like me) that downplaying has no role in a job interview. Sure, don't be a boaster, but you must be in "sell" mode at all times.

Two, be careful of the "informal" associate lunch. It can't win you the job, but it certainly can lose it for you.

Three, remember that we all have stories of failures. I was turned down by more firms than I would like to remember. Take your failures, learn from them, and go rock your next interview.

All it takes is one.

APPENDICES

APPENDIX A: Additional Titles

Dear 1L,

While writing this book, I've consumed hundreds of other books about law school and legal writing. The full list is beyond anything you or any one student might need, so I've distilled it to offer just a handful for you to consider picking up for future reference.

A: Law School:

1. *1L of A Ride* (Andrew McClung)
2. *Law School Confidential* (Robert H. Miller)

B: Exam Success:

    3. *The Eight Secrets of Top Exam Performance in Law School* (Charles H. Whitebread)

    4. *Law School Exams, A Guide to Better Grades* (Alex Schimel)

C: Legal Writing and Communication:

    5. *Legal Writing in Plain English* (Brian A. Garner)

    6. *Making Your Case* (Justice Antonin Scalia; Brian A. Garner)

    7. *Point Made* (Ross Guberman)

    8. *The Winning Brief* (Brian A. Garner)

    9. *Elegant Legal Writing* (Ryan McCarl)

Fondly,

~Amanda

APPENDIX B: Grammar Glossary

A: Parts of Speech

The parts of speech are the basic categories of words in language.

Here are the five that come up often in the types of writing mistakes law students make:

1. Noun: A noun is a word that names a person, place, thing, or idea. Examples include "cat," "pencil," "London," and "love."

2. Pronoun: A pronoun is a word that takes the place of a noun in a sentence. Examples include "he," "she," "it," "they," and "we."

- It will be imperative this year that you make sure your

pronouns properly correspond with the nouns you intend. Learn the pronoun rule now and never forget it:

- A pronoun refers back to the closest noun of the same gender (e.g., he vs. she vs. it) and the same number (i.e., singular vs. plural). Although it's easy to match pronouns when you write in short, simple sentences, you'll find that as your sentences grow in length and complexity, getting your pronouns right becomes increasingly difficult. If you don't "see" instantly that a group of students is an "it" rather than a "they," for instance, you'll want to sharpen your skills before law school starts.

3. Verb: A verb is a word that expresses action, occurrence, or state of being. Examples include "walk," "happen," and "be."

- State-of-being verbs are considered "weak" because they don't serve to propel your sentences forward. You'll want to use action verbs over state-of-being verbs in legal writing this year.

4. Adjective: An adjective is a word that modifies or describes a noun or pronoun. An adjective provides more information about the qualities or characteristics of the word it modifies. Examples include "yellow," "cheerful," and "bright."

5. Adverb: An adverb is a word that modifies or describes a verb, an adjective, or another adverb, often indicating manner, time, place, degree, or frequency. Examples include "quickly," "very," and "often."

In legal writing, you'll want to use stronger verbs and adjectives that don't need adverbs to infuse them with life. Consider writing "famished" or "starving," instead of "very hungry," for instance.

PS—There are also three other parts of speech, which I mention only for reference:

1. Prepositions (e.g., "in," "above," and "before") show the relationship between a noun or pronoun and other words in the sentence,
2. Conjunctions (e.g., "and," "but," and "because") connect other words, phrases, or clauses within a sentence, and
3. Interjections (e.g., "ouch!") express strong emotion or sentiment and can stand as their own independent sentences.

B. Parts of Sentences

Here's a list of the primary role that words, phrases, and clauses can play in a sentence:

1. Subject: The subject is the noun, pronoun, or noun phrase that acts out the verb or about which something is said. E.g., "The dog" in "The dog quickly chased the ball."

2. Predicate: The predicate is the part of a sentence that contains the verb and words that go with it. The predicate provides info about the subject, such as what the subject is doing or being. E.g., "quickly chased the ball" in "The dog quickly chased the ball."

3. Object: An object is a noun, pronoun, or noun phrase that the subject acts on through the verb. E.g., "ball" in "The dog quickly chased a ball."

4. Dependent Clause: A dependent clause is a group of words that contains both a subject and a verb but cannot stand alone as a complete sentence. E.g., "because he was tired," in "He walked slowly because he was tired."

5. Independent Clause: An independent clause contains both a subject and a verb and can stand alone as a complete sentence. An independent clause expresses a complete thought and does not depend on another clause to make sense. Example: "She ate quickly."

6. Phrase: A phrase does not contain both a subject and a verb and does not express a complete thought. E.g., "under the bed," in "The cat hid under the bed."

Your legal-writing professor will likely refer to these different sections of a sentence this year. Refer back to the above descriptions if you're not sure what's being discussed in class.

APPENDIX C: Sample Memo

MEMORANDUM

TO: Professor
FROM: Student
DATE:
RE: <u>Moose Sullivan: Validity of Inter Vivos Gift Claim</u>

QUESTION PRESENTED

Under [state] law, is there a valid claim to recover a certificate of deposit (CD) from a donor's estate where his words at the time of the alleged gift transfer suggested the gift would take effect upon his death; only he and the donee witnessed the alleged transfer; the donor's name alone appears on the CD; and after the alleged transfer, the CD was stored in a trunk to which both the donor and the donee had access?

BRIEF ANSWER

No. A bequest from a donor to a donee is not a valid inter vivos gift under [state] law unless the donee shows three elements: (1) an unmistakable intent by the donor to permanently relinquish all interest in and control over the subject of the gift ("Intent"); (2) the actual and immediate transfer and delivery of control and dominion over the gift ("Conveyance"); and (3) the acceptance of the gift by the donee ("Acceptance"). Here, the donee cannot show Intent because the donor's words suggested he meant the gift to occur in the future. There was no Conveyance because delivery of the CD was not immediate or irrevocable where the CD remained in the donor's custody, bore only his name, and was stored in a trunk that he owned and could access. Last, the donee cannot establish Acceptance where he cannot show he ever took possession of the CD. A claim to recover the CD would therefore likely fail.

FACTS

The firm represents Moose Sullivan in a potential suit to recover a CD from the estate of his late brother, Davis Sullivan. Moose took care of Davis during his battle with a rare blood disorder over the last two years of his life. When Davis's illness made it difficult for him to live alone, he even moved in with Moose, who then cared for Davis and tried to ensure that his last days were comfortable.

Davis died on March 1, 2020. Per his 2010 will, Kerri Blue (sister of Davis and Moose) is the estate administrator, and the entire estate is left to charity. Moose seeks to recover a CD from the estate that bears a face value of $100,000.

According to Moose, Davis wanted to repay Moose and his wife for all they had done. Thus, one day Davis asked Moose to get the trunk that held Davis's financial records. Moose retrieved it from the corner of Davis's room and opened it with the combination Davis had shared back in 2016 (when Moose began taking care of Davis's taxes). Davis then rummaged through the trunk, retrieved the CD, and told Moose, "You and Ann can use this to do something nice for yourselves. I know it has been hard taking care of me for the last few years, and you should go to Europe, remodel the beach house, whatever, when I'm not here anymore."

Although Moose owned his own safe deposit box, he chose to leave the CD in Davis's trunk. Moose has explained, "I decided it was smart to leave the CD in the trunk for now to keep it safe." Only immediate family members and hospital staff entered Davis's room, and per Moose, only he and Davis knew the lock combination.

A few days after Davis's memorial, Moose and Blue were going through Davis's trunk when Moose took out the CD. He mentioned the above-referenced conversation with Davis and requested that he receive the CD. Blue refused. She explained that as administrator of Davis's estate, she had a duty to act only according to what the will stated, and the will said nothing about Moose receiving the CD.

DISCUSSION

Moose should not have a viable claim to recover the CD from the estate because the alleged gift of the CD was not a valid inter vivos gift under [state] law.

A valid inter vivos gift claim requires proof of Intent, Conveyance, and Acceptance. As to Intent, the alleged donee must show that the donor "clearly and unmistakably meant to permanently relinquish all interest in and control over the object of the gift." [cite] For Conveyance, there must be an "actual transfer" by the donor of "all right and dominion over" the gift, and the gift should go into effect "immediately and completely" such that "there can be no locus poenitentiae." [cite w/ definition]. Finally, for Acceptance, there must be an "acceptance [of the gift] by the donee, or by some competent agent." [cite] The claimant's burden on all three elements is "clear and convincing evidence," because courts are "mindful of the ease with which," after the ostensible donor is deceased, "fraudulent claims of ownership may be based on made-up gifts of the donor's property." [cite]

Under these standards, a court would likely decide that the alleged gift of the CD from Davis to Moose was not a valid inter vivos gift under [state] law.

A. <u>Intent</u>

When a donor is deceased, Intent is not shown where he did not express a present-tense intention to convey a gift before he died. [Alpha, Beta, Cappa] Applying this rule here, Moose should be unable to show Intent because Davis is now deceased and the words he used when discussing the CD did not evince a present-tense intention to depart permanently with the CD before he died.

There is no inter vivos gift claim when the donor is deceased and the words they used when giving the gift did not evince an intent to depart permanently and irrevocably with the gift at that time. [Alpha]. There, because the donor had passed away shortly after the alleged gift exchange, the court found it necessary to weigh the evidence with "great caution" to ensure the existence of every element of an inter vivos gift. [cite] The court explained that in such a case, the exact words the donor used at the time of the alleged gift were instructive. [cite] The key witness in Alpha, the donee's mistress, stated that the donor said to the donee, "I want you to have everything that's in that big box of financial stuff, and you will have to take care of the budget for a while." [cite] The court reasoned that these words essentially said two things and were thus "far from [showing] clear and unmistakable [intent]." [cite] Accordingly, the court ruled for the donor's estate on the grounds that no valid inter vivos gift had occurred. [cite]

The court reached a similar conclusion in Cappa, where a patient on the way to a detox center had handed his keys to his friend while saying, "You should really have my Porsche. I clearly won't be driving it anywhere." [cite] The court ruled that the use of "should" suggested either a future or temporary intent "as much as it suggested any permanent one." [cite] The court explained, "If the transfer is to be for an indefinite, short-term period, it is only a promise without consideration and cannot be enforced either at law or in equity." [cite] Concluding that the patient's words were too vague to connote a "permanent, present-tense donative intent," the court dismissed the donee's inter vivos gift claim. [cite]

As in <u>Alpha</u> and <u>Cappa</u>, a court should consider Davis's words ambiguous. According to Moose, Davis said, "You and Ann can use this to do something nice for yourselves. I know it has been hard taking care of me for the last few years, and you should go to Europe, remodel the beach house, whatever, when I'm not here anymore." These words could be construed multiple ways. <u>See</u> <u>Alpha</u>. [cite] Davis's inclusion of the phrase "when I'm not here anymore" suggests that he did not mean for the gift to occur immediately, but upon his death in the future—very much like the words of the <u>Alpha</u> donor. [cite] Davis's words also mimic those used in <u>Cappa</u>: Davis's "when I'm gone" could be interpreted as meaning "during the time Davis was in the hospital," and Davis's "[you] can use [the alleged gift]" connotes no more permanency than the <u>Cappa</u> donee's "[y]ou should have [the alleged gift]" language. [cite] Given the factual similarities between <u>Alpha</u>, <u>Cappa</u>, and this case, a court would likely decide that Davis's intention was not clear and that Moose therefore cannot establish Intent.

That Moose knew the combination to Davis's trunk should not change the result. A similar circumstance presented in <u>Beta</u>, where a donor with a type of cancer described as a "death sentence" had handed a donee the keys to the donor's safe deposit box while uttering, "I'm in the hospital. You should hold on to this. It's yours." [cite] After that, the donor miraculously recovered and left the hospital, but when the donee visited her at home and mentioned the keys, the donor said, "It's OK. You need it more than I do." [cite] Although the court ultimately ruled for the donee, in doing so, the court stated, "Mere delivery of the key does not necessarily indicate an intent to part permanently with control." [cite] The court explained that the donor's delivery of the key might have meant only that the donee should have access to the safe's contents during the donor's hospital stay. [cite] Ultimately, however, the court decided that the donor's second set of words dispelled the confusion. [cite] As a result, the court concluded that the donee could show Intent. [cite]

Beta is distinguishable on its facts. Although Davis's giving Moose the trunk combination resembles the donor's giving the donee the safe-box keys in Beta, that is not enough to establish Intent. [cite] Indeed, Davis did not provide the trunk combination in connection with the alleged gift. Rather, he gave Moose the combination years earlier to allow him to assist with Davis's financial matters. Unlike in Beta, moreover, there was no second set of words to indicate that Moose could keep the CD. See id. These facts make the outcome of the Beta court inapplicable here, and given the totality of cases, a court would likely distinguish Beta and rule against Moose on the Intent issue.

B. Conveyance

A court should reach the same result on Conveyance. To make a gift inter vivos perfect and complete, there must be "an actual transfer of all right and dominion over it by the donor." <u>Llama</u> [cite]. The law also does not permit an inter vivos gift where "a power of revocation or dominion over the subject of the gift" is reserved to the donor, either expressly or due to circumstances. <u>Id.</u> Under these standards, Moose's attempt to establish Conveyance would likely fail because there was no delivery of the CD to his possession.

The <u>Llama</u> case shows that without delivery of the gift to the donee, there can be no valid inter vivos gift. [cite] {Alternate Topic Sentence: No valid inter vivos gift occurs when the donor does not deliver the alleged gift to the donee. [cite]} The court in <u>Llama</u> ruled that although the donor had expressed sufficient Intent to make an inter vivos gift, because she never followed through with delivery of the gift, the donee had no valid claim to it. [cite] The <u>Llama</u> donor had told the donee, "I am gifting you the antique coins I keep in my closet. They represent the past, and I am moving on. Come over so I can give them to you." [cite] After saying that, however, the donor fell asleep and never awoke. [cite] When the donee arrived the next day to collect the coins, the donor's grieving mother pushed him back and slammed the door. [cite] In the donee's case against the estate to recover the coins, the court held that even though the donor's intention seemed "clear," absent any actual transfer of the coins "to the donee's possession," there could be no valid inter vivos gift under state law. [cite] A court would likely follow the reasoning of <u>Llama</u> and decide that like the donee there, Moose never had the CD in his possession and thus cannot establish Conveyance.

Moreover, even though the courts in <u>Delta</u> and <u>Epsilon</u> decided in favor of donees on Conveyance, a court facing our facts should view those cases as off-point. In <u>Delta</u>, the donors were the donee's parents, and they alleged they had maintained control over a gift because the donee had returned it to them to keep in their safe deposit box. <u>Id.</u> The record showed, however, that the donee "was in possession of the coins for some period of time" after the original delivery, and that he kept them "in his room and regularly took them out to show them off to his friends." <u>Id.</u> These facts led the court to rule for the donee on Conveyance. [cite] Likewise, in <u>Epsilon</u>, a case factually like <u>Delta</u>, the court held that "where an actual delivery to a donee occurs, a return back to the alleged donor, when he or she is acting as the donee's agent for a restricted purpose, does not impair the validity of the gift." [cite]

Unlike in <u>Delta</u> and <u>Epsilon</u>, however, the evidence here does not show that Davis ever relinquished complete control over the CD or that Moose ever had possession of it. That means there was never any initial delivery of the CD, such that there also could not have been any return of that CD back to the donor for a specific or limited purpose, as occurred in <u>Delta</u> and <u>Epsilon</u>. Indeed, Moose has admitted, "I decided it was smart to leave the CD in the trunk for now to keep it safe." [cite] That suggests a situation of locus poenitentiae, in that Davis, by way of circumstance, had now retained control over the subject of the gift and, in the future, he could withdraw any promise he might have made to part with it. <u>See</u> [cite]. These facts preclude Moose from establishing Conveyance.

C. <u>Acceptance</u>

Moose should be unable to show Acceptance for the same reasons he cannot show Conveyance: Without delivery of the CD to Moose, there could be no acceptance of the CD by Moose. Indeed, after holding that Conveyance had not occurred, the <u>Llama</u> court declined to address Acceptance as "moot." [cite] Given the similarities between <u>Llama</u> and this case (detailed above), a court might do the same here.

Even were the Conveyance element met, moreover, a court is not apt to find Acceptance because neither Moose nor anyone on his behalf ever had complete possession of the CD. That renders irrelevant the holding in <u>Zeta</u>, where the court ruled for a donee and held that Acceptance occurred "when the donee's son put the gift in his car and drove away." [cite] Unlike in <u>Zeta</u>, no actual retrieval of the CD by Moose or anyone acting on his behalf occurred. In fact, it is Moose's own testimony that leaves unclear whether Moose ever had the CD in his hands, let alone his valid possession. He thus should be unable to show Acceptance.

CONCLUSION

Any claim by Moose to recover the CD on an inter vivos gift theory should fail on three grounds. First, Davis's words at the time of the alleged transfer did not evince an unmistakable intent to make the CD an immediate gift. Second, there was no relinquishment of complete control over the CD, much less an immediate one. Third, Moose could not have accepted something that was not delivered to him or someone on his behalf. Moose thus cannot prove any of the three prerequisites to a viable inter vivos gift claim. An attempt to recover the CD under an inter vivos gift theory should therefore fail.

APPENDIX D: Global Cheat Sheet

1. "Judgement." Doesn't exist in legal writing. Spell it "judgment." (Ch 2.5)

2. Capitalization of "at." The "a" in "at" should never be capitalized in citations. (Ch 2.5)

3. Superscript. Lawyers don't use it. Write 1st, 2nd, 3rd, 4th, etc. (Ch 2.5)

4. Check autocorrections. Tortuous → tortious. (Ch 2.5)

5. Defined terms. After you've defined a term, don't write it out in full again later. (Ch 5.10)

6. Check your headings. Make sure they're actually centered. (Ch 5.13)

7. Capitalization of "court." In an office memo, capitalize "court" ONLY when referring to (1) a court by its full, proper name, or (2) the US Supreme Court. (Ch 6.1)

8. "In the case at bar" and "in that case." Use "here" and "there." (Ch 6.2)

9. "They" for "company." Change to "it." (Ch 6.3)

10. Punctuation with quotes. Periods and commas go INSIDE the quotes; semicolons and question marks go after (unless they are in the original that you're quoting). (Ch 6.4)

11. Oxford and TICTAC commas. Use consistently throughout. (Ch 6.6)

12. Punctuation with "Id.," The period IS underlined. The comma is NOT. (Ch 6.8)

13. "Cite to" doesn't exist. Change to "cite." (Ch 6.9)

14. Mismatched pronouns. A pronoun links back to the closest preceding noun of the same number (i.e., singular vs. plural) and gender (he vs. she vs. it). (Ch 6.10)

15. Mystery facts. Make sure all factual details in your discussion section have already been described neutrally in your facts section. (Ch 6.10)

16. Block quotes. Use sparingly, if at all, but if you do use, the ending citation goes FLUSH LEFT, double-spaced below the quote. The citation should not be indented.

17. Missing rulings. For the cases you use for compare/contrast purposes, always state which side won on the operative issue. (Ch 9.3)

18. "As such." Don't use it. It does NOT mean "Therefore." (Ch 10.4)

19. "Is comprised of" and "is comprised by." Do not exist. (Ch 10.5)

20. "Utilize." Don't use it to mean "use." Write "use." (Ch 11.6)

21. Follow the Terminator Rule. Change "terminate her" to "terminate her employment." (Ch 10.6)

22. Check "however." Consider "But" or "Yet" to start a sentence. (Ch 11.3)

23. "Prior to" and "subsequent to." Change to "before" and "after." (Ch 11.5)

24. "While" vs. "although." "Although" is clearer. (Ch 11.4)

25. "Since" vs. "because." Stick with "because." (Ch 11.7)

26. "In order to." Check if "to" works. (Ch 12.3)

27. "The fact that." Check if "that" works. (Ch 12.4)

28. "Is not required to." Consider "need not." (12.5)

29. "Which" vs. "that." A "which" is almost always wrong. (I.2)

30. Excessive adverbs. Find more vivid verbs; use a thesaurus. (I like OneLook.) (I.3)

***

Acknowledgments

Thank you to Matt for reading so many of my early LinkedIn posts in real time and for being my "encourager superior" throughout, and to Mom, for everything else.

Thank you to Gregory Parker, Julia Torres, and Diliana Gresbrink, who each "got into the weeds" with me to provide longterm, invaluable support at several stages along the way and whose contributions are what ultimately made this book more useful for all readers.

Thank you to my additional beta readers, Teresa Levesque, Nate Crespo, Ted Gomes, and Dylan Brower, who gave me insightful feedback, suggestions for improvement, and words of enthusiasm, all of which helped improve key aspects of this book.

Thank you to John Espirian, my trusted LinkedIn and personal branding coach, and thank you to Kenn Schroder, my longtime website manager/book coach, who both believed in me and this book long before I did, and who carried me through many trying times.

Thank you to every member of the publishing squad I gathered to help me through the amazing Rising Authors platform and community, headed by the generous Hussein al-Baiaty, especially Marie Kuipers and A. J. Hendrickson, my proofreaders; Jason Arias, my book and interior layout designer; Ami Hendrickson, my copywriter; and Christian Dufner, my production editor.

Thank you to all the friends and colleagues who helped me in unique, priceless ways throughout the process, especially:

- Ross Guberman, for his unbridled generosity to me over the past three years and for a friendship I cherish;
- Jordana Confino, for entering my world at precisely the moment I needed her and for providing the type of unconditional support that only she knows how to provide;
- Laura Frederick, for being such an enthusiastic role model and for publishing her own book, *How to Contract*, which gave me a roadmap early on in my process of developing this one;
- Mark Fava, for being my first-time-author sanity saver and friend, for referring me to Rising Authors, and for assuring me that everyone else struggles with the "Author" label, too;
- Jay Harrington, for being one of the first to teach me about how to approach writing a book for self-publication,

and whose thought leadership originally inspired my early LinkedIn posts;

- Alex Su, for generously sharing his time with me and for recommending Rob Fitzpatrick's *Write Useful Books*, which ultimately became the framework and focus for this book; and

- Heidi Brown and Esperanza Franco, for generously reaching out to speak with me to share all their own publishing experiences and to offer their marketing support and encouragement.

Thank you to all members of the law-school classes of 2024 (my "OGs"), 2025, and 2026 (where not mentioned above), especially Cassie Dmitri, Renee Austin, Stephanie Timko, James Scaglione, Alex Bellow, Kyle Brookover, Mason Borneman, Jonathan Koehler, David Schlieffers, Davit Sargsian, Amanda Freeman, Trevin Crider, Hayley Parenti, KimberMarie Faircloth, and AnnaLisa Hamman. I am surely forgetting many of you, for which I apologize. Please know that without the support from each one of you, the original posts giving rise to this book might never have been written.

And finally, thank you to my special group of parents of law students, whose unprecedented enthusiasm and encouragement often served as my only light in the storm, especially Nancy Murphy Brink Moses, Susan Mabry Lawrence, Sherene Shez Silverberg, Renata von Koerber, Brian Jernigan, Sharlton Chastain O'Neal, and Marji Hope.